RETHINKING
THE INCOME
GAP

T0316064

RETHINKING THE INCOME GAP

PAUL RYSCAVAGE

Routledge
Taylor & Francis Group

LONDON AND NEW YORK

First published 2009 by Transaction Publishers

2 Park Square, Milton Park, Abingdon, Oxfordshire OX14 4RN
711 Third Avenue, New York, NY 10017

Routledge is an imprint of the Taylor & Francis Group, an informa business

First issued in paperback 2017

Library of Congress Catalog Number: 2008031103

Library of Congress Cataloging-in-Publication Data

Ryscavage, Paul.
  Rethinking the income gap / Paul Ryscavage.
    p. cm.
  Includes bibliographical references and index.
  ISBN 978-1-4128-0823-1 (acid-free paper)
    1. Income distribution—United States. 2. Social stratification—United States. I. Title.
HC110.15R955 2008
339.20973—dc22   2008031103

ISBN 13: 978-1-4128-0823-1 (hbk)
ISBN 13: 978-1-138-51415-7 (pbk)

For my brother

Dr. Jerome James Ryscavage, Jr.

who has always been an inspirational force

in my life.

Contents

List of Tables and Figures

Tables

Figures

Preface

Economic anxiety about the future began rising in the United States in late 2007 and early 2008. The subprime mortgage crisis was producing mounting home foreclosures and disruptions in financial markets. Soaring oil prices, a falling dollar, and a weakening job market also added to the uneasiness. The nation's economic engine had begun to sputter, and growth in the world's largest economy slowed.

"Recession" was the word on the lips of many pundits—and even "depression" could be heard from a few. Were we headed for our ninth economic slump in 50 years? Maybe yes, maybe no--but certainly the economic mood for millions of Americans had turned grim as they coped with the bad economic news.

Obviously, whether or not the economy slips further downward has implications for the nation's income distribution. What will happen to the shape of the distribution—more poor households, a smaller middle class, fewer rich households, or will there be little discernible change? In a year or two, the answer will be known—this is a short-run development.

Changes in the income distribution have been the focus of much media attention in recent decades—the long run. Specifically, the income gap, the more popular name for growing income inequality, has been a long run development. News accounts of mushrooming fortunes, most recently among hedge fund managers and CEOs, alongside reports of a struggling middle class and an intractable poverty class have been common topics in the mainstream media. Their view of *past* income distribution developments has been made crystal clear.

This book is the outcome of an economist's career spent studying and analyzing the nation's income distribution, and his curiosity, as a citizen, with how the nation's media reported and explained past changes that have taken place within that distribution. The idea for the book was sparked by a 1998 symposium on growing income inequality sponsored by the Federal Reserve Bank of Kansas City and held in Jackson Hole, Wyoming. The symposium brought together a distinguished group of economists, bankers, and others interested in the subject.

The speeches and panel discussions at the Jackson Hole symposium were open to the media. Despite the views of these eminent and notable thinkers on the income gap, however, few headlines were made. Indeed, it seemed the big news had been hidden in the shadows of the Grand Teton Mountains which border Jackson Hole. Nevertheless, a reading of the proceedings of this symposium provides one with a glimpse into those shadows and the startling conclusion that the mainstream media virtually ignored: Growing income inequality is *not* a problem!

Alice Rivlin, former Vice Chair of the Board of Governors of the Federal Reserve System and a moderator at the conference, summarized the conclusion this way:

> We've certainly, I think, all agreed poverty, deprivation, and lack of opportunity are things that ought to be of great concern to us, not only as central bankers but in our roles as citizens. There's much less agreement on whether inequality per se, if it isn't associated with an increase in poverty, is a bad thing. [1]

This conclusion confirmed for me and put into words what I had been thinking after many years of rummaging about in the often tedious and arcane literature of income inequality. As a consequence, I was compelled to write this book.

The underlying theme of the book, therefore, is that after years of misuse by the media of the facts surrounding increasing income inequality, we must re-examine what the income gap means and doesn't mean. As will be shown, its relevance as a measure of economic fairness has diminished significantly in recent years—a fact unacknowledged by our media. Instead, the income gap is now linked to a variety of economic problems confronting the nation and used as a rhetorical device for stirring up social concern and advancing political agendas.

A "rethinking" of the income gap is long overdue.

This little book took much time to write. It did so because income inequality is a complicated topic or, as some characterize it, "slippery." It required many visits to libraries, conversations with friends, relatives, and colleagues, as well as an ever watchful eye on the national scene.

I would like to thank especially the American University Library of Washington, DC and the Beaufort County Library of Beaufort, SC for providing me access to their many resources and their help in using them. I would also like to extend a special thanks to the men and women who collect, compile, and analyze the statistics produced by agencies of our Federal government, specifically, the U.S. Bureau of Labor Statistics,

Census Bureau, Congressional Budget Office, and Bureau of Economic Analysis. Only a minute fraction of their output, of course, became a part of my analysis.

Last, I wish to thank three persons who made this book a reality. First, thanks go to Dr. Irving Louis Horowitz, Editorial Director of Transaction Publishers, who was instrumental in my focusing on the book's unifying theme. Second, I thank my brother Jerry—to whom I dedicated this work—since it was he who encouraged me to see it through to completion. And finally, I thank my wife, Karen, who served not only as the sounding board for many of the phrases, sentences, and paragraphs contained herein, but also patiently stood by as I struggled to craft them. It is to her I have the greatest indebtedness.

Any factual errors or misstatements, of course, are all the responsibility of the author.

Note

1.   *Symposium Proceedings: Income Inequality Issues and Policy Options*, A symposium sponsored by the Federal Reserve Bank of Kansas City, Jackson Hole, Wyoming, August 27-29, 1998 (Kansas City: Federal Reserve Bank of Kansas City, 1998), p. 388.

Introduction
You...and the Income Gap!

Whoever controls the media, the images, controls the culture.
—Allen Ginsberg

You...you who just picked up this book are probably neither very rich nor very poor. Yet, something prompted you to spend some time with a book that concerns itself with the growing income differences between the rich and the poor—or, what the mainstream media have come to call, the income gap.

It's because you've heard a lot about this subject in recent years: the rich are getting richer and the poor are just hanging on. And sometimes you (and I) are even included in that other part of the gap: the rich are getting richer and the rest of us—not just the poor—are simply living from paycheck to paycheck.

Although the income gap doesn't make the headlines of the newspapers or the "breaking news" on the cable networks like Iraq and the war on terror, it does catch your attention. And why shouldn't it? Unlike Iraq and terrorist attacks on our country, the income gap has been around for many more years—lurking in the background of the big news like a threatening thug. This is why you picked up the book—that, and because the title says you should be "rethinking" the income gap.

You have been told, even though you're most likely neither rich nor poor, you should be concerned about the growing income gap. Remember Vice President Al Gore telling us back in the year 2000 about the "powerful forces and powerful interests" standing in the way of working families? Remember Senator John Edwards telling us in 2004 about the "two Americas"? Remember the newly elected Senator from Virginia, Jim Webb, telling us, right after President Bush's State of the Union Address in 2007, about the growing chasm that exists between the compensation of our CEOs and the average pay of ordinary workers? Of course, these are all appeals to *your* sense of fairness, economic fairness to be specific. And all Americans want to be fair.

1

Well, if you still have this book in your hands at this point, I'm going to tell you what you're going to learn by continuing to read it. It's going to make you think about, again and again (or rethink), what you have come to believe regarding one of the great social issues of our day—the income gap and economic fairness in America. Indeed, this book will guide you through the process of "rethinking" the income gap and provide you with some news you haven't seen or heard too much about in the mainstream media. Consider it a civic duty to read this book—a duty that has significant implications for the future of our nation.

Our CEOs and Their Image

When the issue of the income gap comes up, what probably immediately pops into your mind is what Senator Jim Webb was talking about: the CEOs of the nation's corporations raking in these huge compensation packages with their multi-million dollar stock options plans, and the Joe Six-Packs who work for these corporations and who are, supposedly, paid nickels and dimes in contrast. Yes, that's the picture you've learned to visualize when you hear those two simple words—income gap.

But let me ask you something. How come you don't bring to mind Tiger Woods and his multi-million dollar prize winnings and the average salary of the local golf pros at the nation's golf courses? Or how about the pay of Alex Rodriguez, the New York Yankees slugger, as compared to the average pay of minor league ball players? Or how about the annual income of Larry King, the evening talk show host, in relation to the average earnings of local television news anchors around the nation?

After you've pondered that for a moment, let me ask you something else. In the place of Tiger Woods, Alex Rodriguez, and Larry King, and their counterparts, substitute some names of personages in similar lines of work from earlier eras in our country's history. How about Ben Hogan, Ted Williams, and Walter Winchell and their counterparts from the 1940s and 1950s? Do you think the incomes of Woods, Rodriguez, and King are the same multiples of their counterparts as the incomes of Hogan, Williams, and Winchell were of their counterparts? I don't. I think they were a whole lot bigger in the early 2000s.

These CEOs we keep hearing about are supposedly running away with the store, or so many media stories would want you to believe. They set the "stingy" wage policy for their employees while the boards of directors and compensation committees set the CEOs' astronomical compensation packages—even when the companies are losing money and stock prices are heading south.

I would argue that this is simply income gap rhetoric spawned by the nation's mainstream media. Our major papers, magazines, and electronic broadcasters have had a field day reporting the accounts of these CEOs' golden parachutes and their $280 million stock options—indeed, it has become a national pastime for the media to keep tabs on them and it certainly raises questions in the minds of many.

 But in reality, how many of these "assaults on fairness" have there been? Is it the norm or the exception? More generally, what have all these "meany" CEOs done to you? And taken collectively, what have they done for you and your country? Let me tell you.

CEOs lead, direct, and manage most of the American economy. And I contend they have done a pretty good job. The private sector of the economy has grown from $1.6 trillion in 1975 to $10.3 trillion in 2005 and created over 45.0 million jobs for you, me, and most everyone else.[1] Or do you think your private sector job just sprung up out of the earth? Sure there have been bumps and bruises along the way (i.e., downsizings, restructurings, shutdowns) and there's more to come no doubt. Indeed, the economic clouds darkened in 2007 and early 2008 and confidence in the economy plummeted. With problems in the subprime mortgage market, skyrocketing oil prices, and other unsettling economic developments, Americans were staring at the possibility of another economic recession as of this writing.

But this is a book about *long run* trends in the nation's income distribution and not short run developments. I am confident our CEOs will steer us through the choppy waters as they have before—and 30 years from now in 2038 someone will cite similar or even better economic statistics as I did above reflecting the resilience and dynamism of the American economy.

So how much do you think our CEOs are worth?

In my opinion, they are worth every cent they receive—as long as they've earned it legally! And please don't tell me that in Japan they only make "such-and-such" as much as the average Japanese worker. That's Japan, this is America. Our culture, our economy, our lifestyles, have been formed and molded by different forces. Sure, there probably could be more of a relationship between performance and pay for our CEOs because that's the way our economic system is supposed to run in the first place: You get paid for what you contribute to the economy. But I would suggest that most of our CEOs are being paid for their performance—look at the statistics mentioned above as evidence.

But the income gap rhetoric found in the media resonates with a part of the body-politic because it implies that the CEOs and the corporate types are simply a greedy bunch, living off the hard work of all their underlings. You…you saw the pictures flashing across your television screen of Bernie Ebbers, the head of WorldCom, convicted of fraud and conspiracy, being hauled off to jail, and Jeffrey Skilling and the late Ken Lay of Enron fame, looking down-in-the-mouth and forlorn as they walked from the courthouse after learning of their similar fates. These are hard images to erase—especially when they are linked to the "income gap."

But how come when you hear about the greedy CEOs you don't conjure up the image of Bill Gates of Microsoft or Warren Buffet of Berkshire Hathaway or Donald Trump, the billionaire builder of hotels, casinos, and the TV hit, The Apprentice? These are all very successful corporate leaders with "gazillions" of dollars combined. I will tell you why you don't connect them with the income gap. It's because the media have featured them as "positive" money men: the impression created, in my opinion, is that they are very nice people (which they probably are) because they give their money away and amuse us with TV shows and their antics. Yet, here are financial powerhouses—and from what we know about the world of high finance and big corporations, they are not exactly operating in a "playschool" environment. Still, the mainstream media just wait to hear about the next donation of money they will make or the next financial endeavor they will undertake.

You see, it's all about the image—the image created and recorded by the media, which is then conveyed in earnest to the public…me, and most importantly, you!

A classic example is John Mackey, the CEO and founder of the world's largest organic food store, Whole Foods Market. Here's an enterprise with revenue of $5.6 billion in 2006 and a capitalization of a couple billion more—and he announces to the world that he will take an annual pay of $1. What a guy! Now that's a CEO.

This is a store that Mr. Mackey built, I suspect, with an image in mind. Whole Foods, it just sounds wonderful, organic food, no preservatives—and happy employees, well paid employees—a family, working together for the betterment of society. And the CEO pays himself a buck!

There is no doubt about it that Mackey's Whole Foods Market is a great store. But, and I don't know this as a fact, he too probably had to make some "tough" business decisions along the way. After all, one doesn't just become the largest organic grocery store in the world overnight by being a "pushover." For example, even he had to raise his "management pay-to-average employee pay" differential from 14 to 1 to 19 to 1 to stay abreast of the competition. But, of course, Mr. Mackey quickly apologized in his personal blog to his fans, customers, and the media, pointing out that in today's America the comparable differential is 431 to 1.

Mr. Mackey is smart. This CEO created a business image that won't make you think about *him* and *his* store when the media begin beating up on CEOs. But, unfortunately, even he ran into a bit of an image problem in 2007 in his effort to buy a smaller rival organic grocer. And to the credit of the mainstream media, they did report the story.[2] Apparently, he was "extolling" his company's stock online according to newspaper accounts—and it did get messy for awhile. But, like I said, Mr. Mackey is smart—and this CEO is still floating right on top of the stormy CEO seas.

So, in my opinion, Mr. Mackey knows he deserves to make money (i.e., a profit) and has   with an image—and wants to keep the media at bay, I suppose, just like Bill Gates, Warren Buffett, and Donald Trump.

The Top 1 Percent and Fairness

You have also heard a lot about, along with the CEOs, those rich folks who represent the top 1.0 percent of the household income distribution. These people, and their household members, are the ones who, supposedly, are gobbling up all of the income gains leaving your household and mine—with the crumbs.

To be precise, the top 1.0 percent of all households with the highest incomes would amount to 1.2 million households in 2006 since there were roughly 116 million households in that year.[3] CEOs would most likely be included according to Census Bureau data; the income threshold for the top 1.0 percent of all households would probably be between $250,000 and $300,000, maybe more if it were estimated using other income data.[4] No doubt, many CEOs would be above this threshold. Estimates of the number of CEOs of our largest corporations vary. I've seen one estimate recently of about 14,000 and, of course, it's a "knowable" number since we could count up the number of corporations in the country from the Internal Revenue Service records. But the point is obvious: these CEOs account for only a part of those at the top of the income distribution.

So, who else are we talking about in the top 1.0 percent? It doesn't take much to figure that out. Most likely it's the corporate types who work for the CEOs (i.e., chief financial officers, corporate attorneys, and accountants), the managers of hedge funds and mutual funds, dot-com entrepreneurs, investment bankers, Wall Street lawyers and famous attorneys, independent financiers, securities and commodity traders, highly specialized doctors and surgeons, superstar athletes and entertainers, real estate magnates, "old money" types who have inherited their fortunes, even certain politicians, and on and on. As Ben Stein, the economist, lawyer, author, said in *The New York Times*, these are the people who either help people (especially rich people) make money (e.g., Peter Lynch) or make people feel better (e.g., Eddie Murphy, Phil Mickelson) and most importantly, operate in areas where lots of money is "sloshing" around (e.g., Wall Street, Hollywood, the PGA).[5] He went on to say that it is *not* very likely the top 1.0 percent are composed of many people who majored in nineteenth-century African feminism or Bulgarian poetry.

Some of those worrying about the income gap also refine the top 1.0 percent and point their finger at the very "tipity" top of the income distribution—the top 0.1 percent, or a little more than 100,000 households. Of course, one can quickly tick off the names of a few who are probably here—Bill Gates, Warren Buffett, Donald Trump, Tiger Woods, Oprah Winfrey, and, of course, the very highest paid CEOs and hedge fund managers in the country. Are we really mad at these guys and gals—every single one of those rich folks—you and me? I'm not. And really, they don't add up to a whole lot of people in the first place.

Speaking of you and me, we're down there along with everyone else below the ninety-ninth percentile of the income distribution. We're the ones supposedly getting "worked over" by the system, the system all these fat cats are running. That's what some in the mainstream media are telling us. Even though the media refers to the income gap, they really don't mean just the rich and the poor. They mean the middle class as well. Today, we hear how hard it is to educate the kids, plan for our retirement, provide health insurance for our families—and keep our jobs from being "outsourced." The story is we're being "nickled and dimed" to death—and we're a pretty miserable lot, us folks down here below the ninety-ninth. And now we're looking at a possible recession!

But you...and me...and the rest of us below the ninety-ninth, we're not dopes! We know the rich have gotten richer, *but* so have most of us over recent decades—just not as fast as the very rich. And what's so wrong with that if one believes that one's paycheck or income should reflect in some good measure one's contribution to society?

According to a story in *The New York Times*, it was only those above the ninetieth percentile of the income distribution, and especially those at the ninety-ninth and above, whose incomes rose in 2005, while everyone else's were falling.[6] If looking at a bar graph of income changes across the income distribution, some commentators would have you believe that you wouldn't see any bars until you reached the top end of the income distribution and then there would be this huge, gigantic bar representing the "whopping" income gain for the rich.

But a long run graph I could make with income data from the U.S. Census Bureau or the Congressional Budget Office would provide you with a different picture.[7] Sure, the biggest bar would still be for those at the top, but as you dropped down into the distribution (where you and I are) you'd still find bars representing income gains. They would be smaller and smaller, like a staircase, but they still would represent positive income gains. This is the true reality of the income gap over time.

Indeed, I believe, and I think a lot of us believe, income gains should reflect our contribution to the economy and society—and the "staircase" profile is more representative of economic fairness than everybody getting the same income gain the way those in much of the mainstream media would have it (as well as the true egalitarians of our society). It's fairer because not everyone makes similar contributions as a result of differences in our skill and talent endowments.

The Media and YOUR Perceptions

The media has a long tradition in this country of telling us not only about what is going on, but also of what they believe or what their opinion is about what's going on. Just look at our history. Issues of economic expansion, slavery, war and peace, immigration, poverty, civil rights, have all prompted the media to, not only report the information to us, but also to give us their opinion, whether we like it or not. It's a necessity in a free and democratic country—but it is also a necessity embodying risks and dangers.

Like all of our institutions in this country, from the government to the churches to the corporations to the schools, the media are also susceptible to mistakes, errors, and wrongdoing in carrying out their mission. Sometimes I believe our society gives them, the media, a "pass" or "looks the other way," only because of this "freedom of the press" notion that often clouds our conscience. But when they get it wrong, the consequences can be very serious—for you, for me—because our perceptions are at stake.

The line between reporting information and offering opinion is often fuzzy. Skilled journalists know this. A case in point—and an apropos one—concerns the usage of the terms "income gap" and "income inequality." Each year the U.S. Census Bureau reports on the poverty and income situation in the nation, including a number of statistics that measure *income inequality*. Invariably, when these statistics have indicated an increase in income inequality, the media headlines read "Income Gap Widens."

Why?

"Inequality" and "gap," of course, have different connotations. Inequality is less emotionally charged. No one likes gaps. They are immediately perceived as representing something bad—someone or somebody being cheated or left behind. We see and hear in the media about a variety of gaps: the gender gap, the wage gap, the digital gap, the racial gap, the housing gap, the health insurance gap. In today's society, usage of the term "gap" automatically signals a fairness issue.

Back in the early 1980s, a few government and academic economists discovered that the difference in the annual earnings of workers with low earnings and high earnings had been widening during the previous decades.[8] By the mid-1980s, a small army of economists were examining trends in family and household incomes and finding that inequality was growing among them as well. And so it went, right up to the present time. For the media, all this was compelling news—and as they say, the "rest is history."

In effect, the academic and governmental research into income inequality was "swept up" by the mainstream media of America—and then turned into the income gap. Any implicit moral overtones found in "income inequality" become explicit when it is referred to as the "income gap."

And income gap stories catch your attention. They do so because they might involve you, especially because of the way we have come to think of (thanks to the media) the income gap. When we have read or heard about the income gap in the past there was this automatic linkage to the other dominant economic stories of the day: The ever-present news stories about job security and outsourcing, health insurance coverage, under-funded pensions, education costs, and all the other so-called threats to economic life in America.

The fallout from all these stories can be looked at this way: First, a large segment of Americans have not "bought into" the stories because economic times haven't been bad for them in the past, indeed, the times couldn't have been better. They were buying vacation homes, two or three cars, sending the children to Europe for their second semester, taking exotic vacations and long weekend trips to Las Vegas or Atlantic City, and so on. Consequently, what they read in the paper or saw on television about an unfair economy did not really register.

Another segment of Americans, however, have "bought into" the barrage of news stories and television specials about how the income gap was dragging our nation down, as reflected in the above mentioned stories. These people (and they might not only be from the poor, but from the middle class or even the rich) are doubtful about whether or not the economy is on the right track. They questioned whether or not economic justice was being served in this country. For them, the nation had truly become one of "the haves and the have nots."

And yet for a last segment of Americans—a very large segment—there was simply confusion and bewilderment over the income gap issue and the media stories linked to them. This was because their economic lives weren't really all that bad (like the first group above) even though they may have had to "pinch pennies" now and then. They continued to have hopes and dreams of improving their economic lot in life. In short, their reality was out of "synch" with what they read and heard in the media, or their perception. For these people, the income gap issue had turned into the income gap "muddle."

The most unfortunate consequence of the income gap issue for our society today, of course, has been the suspicion, doubt, distrust, and other negative feelings it has engendered—and is engendering—among members of our society towards other members of our society. It has become a divisive issue, much like Iraq, the war on terror, globalization, and all the other issues of the day that are nagging at our social conscience. And the pity of it is—it need not be.

You…and This Book

It doesn't matter if you already agree with my point of view—read it because it will, most likely, put into words what you've been thinking for a long time. For those of you who are not sure of my point of view, I encourage you also to plunge ahead. Hear me out. Read and then think about everything you've read and heard before about the income gap—from our mainstream media. And for those of you who are utterly opposed to my point of view, I can only say good-bye and farewell, but remember, you too are part of this economic system.

The book is divided into three sections. The first three chapters discuss how several decades ago a subject of purely academic and scholarly interest—income inequality—was popularized by the mainstream media and turned into a "muddled" national issue for many Americans. This issue, now called the income gap, has been tossed, turned, and twisted like a rag doll by both the political left and the political right and dropped at the doorsteps of each and every one of us.

Chapter 1 deals specifically with the "income gap muddle" and how many Americans are in that muddle. A few examples of how the mainstream media feeds the income gap muddle are presented. Chapter 2 provides a clinicians look at "true" income inequality—the stuff the economists and other researchers first became interested in, or re-interested in, some thirty or forty years ago. It also discusses what these income inequality statistics truly mean in terms of economic fairness. This sets the stage for Chapter 3: a discussion of how we understand what economic fairness means today and how it got that way. The emphasis here is on the nation's cultural past and its evolution since the 1960s.

The second section of the book brings you, the reader, front and center with the income inequality—economic fairness "disconnect," or why the income gap rhetoric of the mainstream media hasn't caught on with the American middle class any more than it has. This is where the real economic news has been made.

In Chapter 4, the traditional "inverse" relationship between increasing income inequality and decreasing economic fairness is put under the microscope and shown to have broken down during the last few decades. It is posited that a disconnect developed because the economic lives of most everyone in the United States improved to varying degrees over these years because of the wealth creating capability of America's free market, capitalistic system. Chapters 5 and 6 focus on the country's middle class and argues that it is neither in decline nor is it ready to collapse—despite economic recessions now and then. Rather it has "morphed" in recent years both downward and upward. In fact, in recent decades we have been experiencing America's second middle class revolution—the news that the mainstream media neglected to tell you.

The concluding chapters (Chapter 7 and 8) are prescriptive. They confront the presumed ethical question that exists between the distribution of income and the economic foundations of our country. So much of today's income gap rhetoric coming from the mainstream media, if followed to its logical conclusion, would require major changes in the way our economy functions so as to further redistribute income among households. Exorbitant tax rates on the upper middle class and rich, more restrictive corporate regulations (including higher taxes), higher trade tariffs, more centralized economic planning, in short more governmental intervention into the free market, would all be in our future—and their deleterious effects would soon begin crippling the *corpus Americana*.

Once you have completed this little book, ask yourself the simple question: Is the income gap really as unfair as the mainstream media make it out to be, or have we been led astray?

Notes

1. *Economic Report of the President,* February 2006, Table B-12, p. 296, and Table B-46, p. 336.
2. Andrew Martin, "Whole Foods Executive Used Alias," *The New York Times*, July 12, 2007, pp. C1, C5.
3. *Income, Poverty, and Health Insurance Coverage in the United States: 2006* (P60-233), U. S. Bureau of the Census, HHES Division (Washington, DC: USGPO, August, 2007), Table A-1, p. 29.
4. U.S. Census Bureau (*http://www.census.gov*), Income, Detailed Income Tables, Households, Table HINC-06.
5. Ben Stein, "Everybody's Business; You Can Complain, or You Can Make Money," *The New York Times* (Business), Oct. 15, 2006, p. 3.
6. David Cay Johnson, "Income Gap Is Widening, Data Shows," *The New York Times,* March 29, 2007, pp. C1 and C10.
7. *Income, Poverty, and Health Insurance Coverage in the United States: 2006* (P60-233), U.S. Bureau of the Census, Table A-3, pp. 39-40, and *Historical Effective Federal Tax Rates: 1979-2005,* Congressional Budget Office, December 2007, Table 1C.
8. For example, Peter Henle and Paul Ryscavage, "The Distribution of Earned Income Among Men and Women, 1958-77," *Monthly Labor Review,* April, 1980, pp. 3-10.

1

The Income Gap "Muddle"

Perplexity is the beginning of knowledge.
—Kahlil Gibran

Yes, the verdict is in: *income inequality* has increased over the last few decades. Indeed, there is more certainty about this than there is global warming. But please note, I said "income inequality" and not "income gap."

This chapter is about the income gap and how it was turned into the income gap muddle. Before I get to that, however, you need to read a few words about income inequality—from a smart man, with a tough job.

Ben S. Bernanke is the Chairman of the Federal Reserve Board—he's in charge of our country's banking system. In early 2007 he gave a speech in which he summarized the primary causes of growing income inequality.[1] He mentioned three: skill-biased technological change, globalization, and certain institutional changes, such as, declining union membership and erosion of the Federal minimum wage. He could have mentioned others.

More importantly the Chairman also reviewed the "bedrock principles" underlying America's economic system and our roles in it. First, he said, everyone should have the *opportunity* to be whatever they want to be given one's skills, talents, and abilities. Second, and consistent with the first, everyone's economic *outcome* should be linked to the contributions they make to the nation's economy—and these outcomes need not be equal nor guaranteed to be equal. And third, everyone should receive some economic *insurance* against adverse economic outcomes.

I mention these principles because they are often forgotten by Americans these days—forgotten because of the income gap rhetoric that has riddled much of our public discourse. I also mention them because flowing out of these principles was his answer to those worrying about inequal-

13

ity: "…the challenge for policy is not to eliminate inequality *per se* but rather to spread economic opportunity as widely as possible."

Think about this for a moment. How often have you seen such a message reported in today's mainstream media? Not very often I would suspect. That's because over the years they've equated the words, income inequality, with something negative, something bad, something harmful to American society—and called it the income gap.

The Muddle: How It Came About

You may think now I'm parsing words and engaging in semantics. Let me back off for a moment and use the terms "gap" and "inequality" interchangeably so I can advance into the subject of the chapter (the income gap muddle)—and then you'll see more clearly the significance of the Chairman's words.

As far as I can tell, the first time *The New York Times*—the elite of the mainstream media—used the words "income gap" was in 1962. In an article in their Sunday magazine section, the *Times* printed the following headline, "Is the Income Gap Closed? No!"[2] The article was written by Herman P. Miller, a Census Bureau demographer, but whether he or a *Times'* editor wrote the headline is not known. What is known, however, is that the purpose of the article was to dispel the myth that family incomes in America were "leveling" or becoming more similar—and more importantly, it was meant to sound the alarm that a segment of society was being left behind economically, the poor.

Although this piece of history is dealt with later in the book, it's interesting to note that back then—forty-five or so years ago—some people were concerned, not that income inequality was increasing, but that it was *not* decreasing. As will be discussed, income inequality had been very stable in the 1950s and actually reached its lowest point of the twentieth century during the 1960s.

It should be remembered that it was around this period when national attention was being focused on the poor and the civil rights movement—and it was only a few years later that President Lyndon B. Johnson would launch his War on Poverty. So originally, usage of the words "income gap" immediately brought to mind the poor and poverty, or the lower end of the income distribution.

The writings of Miller and other researchers during the 1960s led to a number of academic and government studies of poverty and the economic conditions of blacks. Indeed, references to the black-white "income gap" became more numerous in the media as well. But again, these particular words were linked very strongly to the poor and down-trodden of American society.

Fast forward to more recent years and mention the words "income gap" to the average man or woman in the street and observe the difference. As already discussed, a very popular response one would hear would concern the "gazillion" dollars the CEOs of the nation's companies are receiving in comparison to the "nickels and dimes" the factory workers are making. Others might tell you about the difficulties the middle class is having in "making ends meet" in contrast to the rich and famous living in Manhattan, Hollywood, and Palm Beach. And still yet others might simply point their fingers at the hedge fund managers on Wall Street and say "That's the income gap!"

So, be clear about two things: First, there is this economic phenomenon referred to in our popular culture called the "income gap," which is generally regarded as a negative or bad thing and whose definition is subject to change; and second, there is "income inequality," a fairly well-defined economic phenomenon studied by economists and other researchers, which has a much less pejorative connotation.

Income Gap vs. Income Inequality...Moral Implications

Words are important. If I was a TV news anchor that broadcast the nightly news and I said, "The nation's income gap widened last year," this would be considered a negative piece of news. But if I had said, "Income inequality in the nation increased last year," it would be considered a less negative piece of news. This is because "gap" is a more potent word than "inequality."

The income gap muddle begins to arise because of this very distinction. The mainstream media has equated "gap and inequality," but as Chairman Bernanke pointed out, inequality, per se, is not necessarily bad. Consider the following example involving a room full of kings. They are all very rich, but King A suddenly becomes five times as rich as Kings B, C, D, and E. As the TV news anchor I could announce that there was a widening "income gap" among the five kings and I bet there would be some people out there in TV-land who would start feeling sorry for Kings B, C, D, and E. But if I had announced that "income inequality" was increasing among the five Kings no one out there in TV-land would really care because they were all kings anyway. In today's America, moral implications are more closely linked to the words "income gap" than to the words "income inequality."

Economic Perceptions vs. Economic Reality...
Income Gap Implications

An income gap muddle is created in the minds of many Americans when economic perceptions and economic reality are out of synch. As we know the media is fond of reporting bad news—and in numerous instances, featuring it. In the case of economic news over recent years, haven't we all heard the following: incomes and wages aren't rising, job growth is anemic, jobs are being sent overseas, health insurance isn't available for everyone, health care and education costs are skyrocketing, pensions are under-funded, the Federal deficit and national debt are out of control, and on and on. Sure, some of these stories have elements of truth to them, but not for everybody in the country, nor even a majority of families and households. But each story can have an effect—an effect that *invites* you and me to believe that the American economy is letting us down and treating us unfairly.

After three decades of this treatment, I contend that many Americans, whether consciously or unconsciously, have rejected this notion that our economic system is a failure, regardless of what the polls say. The reason they have either rejected this notion or have doubts is this: Life has been pretty good in America for the vast majority of us over the last several decades! Sure, there are the nagging economic difficulties—there always are and there always will be.

When one looks at the big, economic picture of the nation back into the last century, the only conclusion that can be reached is that the economy has worked pretty well. Consider some of the evidence:

- The poverty rate in 2006 (12.3 percent) was not much different than it was thirty years earlier.
- Middle-class incomes stretch upwards to a $150,000 a year and probably beyond, with thousands of upper middle class households being created in recent years.
- The rich are more numerous and have flourished like they never did before.

But there are still millions of other Americans for whom the frightening economic news coming from the media has had an impact. For a broad swath of citizens across the land, the rhetoric of the mainstream media has turned the income gap (which long ago was linked only to the poor of this nation) into the income gap muddle. For these folks there is bewilderment and confusion about the rising *income inequality* reported by the Federal Reserve Board Chairman Ben S. Bernanke and other organizations.

Perpetuation of the Income Gap Muddle

The existence of an income gap muddle in our society is not something recently thought up by some wild-eyed, right-wing economist. It has been around for a long time. The muddle usually becomes more palpable as the income gap rhetoric (and associated "bad economic news" stories) is ratcheted up during periods before presidential and congressional elections, and especially economic recessions.

Back in 2006, David Brooks, a columnist for *The New York Times,* sensed its existence in a political context, when he wrote in one of his columns:

> …Democrats have generally conceived of America as a society between comfortable haves and insecure have-nots. Having read thousands of gloomy articles about downsizing, outsourcing and wage stagnation, they've tried to rally the insecure working majority against the privileged minority—or as Al Gore put it, the people against the powerful.
>
> But since this strategy has notably failed, some analysts are thinking maybe there is no frightened majority longing for government succor.[3]

This majority that Brooks refers to no doubt contains many in today's income gap muddle, which we have been discussing. Simply review some of the topics of the past economic news that have helped create it—and perpetuate it every day via the mainstream media:

- Wal-Mart, the employer of workers with low wages and poor benefits
- Immigrant laborers, how we love them, how we hate them
- Haves vs. the have mores, the new class war
- Gilded paychecks, the very rich are leaving the rich behind
- Anxious middle class, families missing out on the benefits of growth
- Money, does it make us happy?
- Auto workers, their "end of the line"

These topics, and others like them, don't have to mention the income gap—it's there, buried in the verbiage. Some of them have merit, of course, when the income gap implications are subtracted out; however, most of them imply that someone or something is to blame. Indeed, the message, the subliminal message if you will, is just that: This is not fair and someone or something must be blamed!

The fact that the mainstream media in our country tilts politically to the left is nothing new, notwithstanding the recent crusades of Bernard Goldberg and others.[4] Over twenty years ago, Ben Wattenberg, from the American Enterprise Institute, a conservative "think tank" in Washington, DC, was making a similar argument about the media.[5]

But it is very evident that the mainstream media's messages in more recent years, which I've pointed to, also have had their affect. According to a Pew Research Center survey in 2007, the percentage of respondents that agreed with the proposition that "the rich just get richer and the poor get poorer" rose from 65 percent in 2002 to 73 percent in 2007 (this was slightly below the high of 80 percent in 1991, however, when the economy was in a recession).[6]

Furthermore, *The New York Times* in early 2007 reported a revealing story reflecting the effect of the income gap rhetoric.[7] A judge in Chicago was having difficulty in forming a jury for the trial of the Canadian press tycoon Conrad M. Black. One of the sticking points was the responses potential jurors were giving to the question about individuals who are being paid "tens of millions of dollars." Even though the judge advised the jury pool there was nothing wrong with making a lot of money, many of the potential jurors disagreed. "I don't think that anyone should get that amount of money from any company," said one juror, and another said, "When I hear tens of millions of dollars, I shudder." An implication in the *Times* story, was that the memories of Enron, WorldCom, and other corporate scandals was a factor.

Obviously, words—like income gap—are important.

Three Specific Examples

Among the thousands and thousands of media stories I could have picked to illustrate my point, I believe three stand out. They stand out because one comes from one of the stars of the electronic media and the other two from the stars of the elite print media—and each of these stories focus on different parts of the income distribution.

Before I get to them, it is important to realize a common characteristic in all of these stories that fuel the income gap muddle. As pointed out earlier, the income gap contains moral and ethical implications. Who is to blame for the low wages, the lost or nonexistent health insurance, the under-funded pensions, the jobs going to other countries? In other words, "blame" is implicit in all of these stories and it must be affixed to someone, something. Now, in the case of Enron and WorldCom and the other examples of corporate malfeasance, the blame is very obvious. But in most of the other stories, blame or culpability, if it is to be parceled out, is a matter of debate—at least in my opinion. The mainstream media, however, have a way of implying blame. So, when you come across these stories, be on the lookout for the victim (who will always be made explicit) and the culprit (who, usually but not always, will only be implied).

First Example. Don Imus is the popular talk show host of "Imus in the Morning." He got himself into a lot of trouble (indeed, he lost his job) in the spring of 2007 because of his remarks about the Rutgers University women's basketball team.

As you might know, his demeanor is typically gruff and prone to ranting about this and that which annoys him. He frequently interviews famous politicians, entertainers, writers, country and western singing stars, and so on.

I watched him from time-to-time on MSNBC and sometimes enjoyed his humor (along with that of his support staff—Charles, Bernie, Lou, and the others). He sometimes made the front pages of the elite newspapers and was mentioned in the nightly news when he interviewed someone in the national limelight, like Senator John McCain or Vice President Dick Cheney. So, Imus provides a mixture of serious public discourse with musical performances and hard-edged humor. This is his "thing."

The following is an example (less egregious than the Rutgers incident) of his commentary, but this time it was in the context of the income gap. A couple years ago I was watching and listening to one of his early morning shows and I picked up my ears when he began expounding about Wal-Mart. Basically, his complaint, which by this time was becoming fairly standard fare for the elite media, was this: it was wrong for the Wal-Mart Corporation to pay its workers so poorly and provide such lousy benefits, especially when Wal-Mart sold low-priced products made in China that should have been made in this country in the first place by our own workers for much higher wages.[8]

As a labor economist, my ears reddened (after they picked up) because here was a highly popular figure taking a "poke" at one of this nation's (indeed, world's) more successful corporations that employs 1.4 million workers. Certainly, Imus had a right to his opinion. But Wal-Mart has probably *helped* to improve the economic well-being of more Americans via its "always low prices" marketing program than any other corporation in the country.

Obviously, Don Imus frequently "walked a tightrope" when he was into one of his commentaries. In the case of Wal-Mart, I asked myself: Had he ever run a cost-benefit analysis of the Wal-Mart Corporation as to the economic welfare it provided American households and its employees, or was he just "doing his thing?"

In this particular instance, Imus did not mention the income gap. He didn't have to. I think his audience could figure out who the victims were—and who the culprit was. This was perpetuation of the income gap muddle, in my opinion.

My answer to the charges that Wal-Mart's wage and benefit packages are unfair is this: If indeed their labor compensation package is so unfair, why haven't their 1.4 million employees quit and looked for other jobs? Might it be because they are good jobs for the kinds of jobs they are?

But, as most of us have heard, Imus is back on-the-air and, presumably, continues to offer his opinions about this and that once again.

Second Example: A month or so before the 2004 Presidential election, *The Washington Post* ran a story on the front page with a headline that read, "As Income Gap Widens, Uncertainty Spreads," and the sub-headline read, "More U.S. Families Struggle to Stay on Track."[9]

This article, I suspect, was motivated by politics since the election was only six weeks away and there was no special event (i.e., release of survey results, study, or analysis of income inequality data) that had occurred that could have prompted it. Unlike the Don Imus example, the author of the *Post* article explicitly referred to the income gap.

The article was about the middle class and how job losses were causing its erosion (again, note how the income gap now includes the middle class). In a long and detailed description, the author told how two or three individuals from the state of Virginia had lost their jobs because of plant closings and could only find lower paying jobs to support their families. Statistics and graphics were presented relating to the household income distribution in the nation, based on Census Bureau information. In a neighboring box, the *Post* said, "This is the first in an occasional series about the changes roiling the middle of the American workforce--."

Because of my interest in income inequality as well as the article's use of Census Bureau data, I read the story very carefully. To say the least, this was a depressing and frightening article. It clearly gave the impression that jobs typically held by the middle class were disappearing and that the country's middle class was "hollowing out" thereby creating an even wider income gap.[10]

The disappearance of the middle class has been much debated by academics and politicians alike. It is not a new issue. Changes taking place in the middle class have been related to the transformation of the skill and education needs of employers as the economic structure of the nation shifts from goods-production to one of producing services and information.[11] In addition, the changes occurring to the middle class are related to the shifts that have taken place in the composition of our families and households (i.e., single-parenting, divorce, and marital breakup).[12]

This particular *Post* article is a classic example of an effort by the elite media to perpetuate the income gap muddle. There are a number of reasons. First, the article defined middle class as households with annual incomes in the "income class" of $35,000 to $49,999—and the *Post* author showed how the proportion of households in this class declined over time, presumably because of job loss. But if the middle class is defined to contain households with incomes up to $99,999, the picture of the middle class would be one of stability. And if it were defined as rising all the way up to $149,999 (where I suggest the upper middle class income range begins to end), the *Post* story would have had to talk about an "expansion" of the middle class!

A second reason is when the author ascribed the decline in middle class households (in the income range of $35,000 to $49,999) to the disappearance of middle class jobs. For every person mentioned in this article that was caught in the gears of our market economy and ended up with low-paying jobs, thousands of others found high-paying jobs and moved further up into the middle class, as my definition of the middle class would show. Moreover, the demographic profile of this narrow income range no doubt shifted markedly in recent years. Married-couple families are proportionally fewer and single-parent families greater, thereby reducing the potential number of dual earner families and enhanced household incomes.

The third and most alarming reason is its characterization of our nation's labor market—like a monstrous dragon (called the capitalistic, free market system) gobbling up middle class households and creating a wider income gap. The truth is that between the mid-1990s and 2004, income inequality did not change very much according to Census Bureau reports. Even when the middle class is defined narrowly, the proportion of households in the $35,000 to $99,999 range was between 44 and 46 percent—not exactly a hollowing out. Indeed, between 2003 and 2004, the Bureau reported: "The Gini index, one of the most widely used inequality measures, indicated no change in household income inequality between 2003 and 2004."[13]

The intent of the article was clear. It was not necessarily to inform. Most people knew that the job market in those years had become very challenging and unforgiving if one did not bring to it something that was needed by the employer. In my opinion, the article scared potential voters who were bearing witness to anemic employment growth during this period—and to perpetuate the income gap muddle.

The entire *Post* article could have been written from other perspectives rather than the income gap. It could have been written from the perspective of how skills and educational demands of employers are continually changing or what will be the kinds of jobs and occupations that employers will need in the future. Or the perspective could have been about the training and retraining needs of American workers. But no, the perspective they chose was the income gap, automatically requiring the reader to look for a victim—and, of course, a culprit.

Third Example: The last example of a news story that helps fuel the income gap muddle comes from the *The New York Times* in early 2007.

The story was headlined, "Income Gap Is Widening, Data Shows." It reported to readers the results of an updating of research by two economists who have been studying trends in income concentration in the top part of the income distribution—from the ninetieth percentile and upward, with special attention to the top 1 percent.[14] The *Times* story led with the news that in 2005 the "top 1 percent" of Americans (whose incomes begin at $348,000) received their largest share of national income since 1928. The fifth paragraph added that these economists now estimated that the top 300,000 Americans enjoyed almost as much income as the bottom 150 million other Americans. One of the researchers was quoted: "If the economy is growing but only a few are enjoying the benefits, it goes to our sense of fairness."

The research of Professors Emmanuel Saez and Thomas Piketty has been frequently seen in the media and well received among income inequality researchers. Saez and Piketty have published a number of academic papers concerning their work. One of these papers provides some needed perspective for the *Times* article.[15] According to it, the basic objective of their research was to construct a "homogeneous" statistical series on the income shares received by those persons at and above the ninetieth percentile of the income distribution from 1913 to 2002 so as to observe long run trends in income inequality. And they have done just that.

The source of their income data was individual tax returns from the Internal Revenue Service (IRS). Over the years, the IRS published summarizations of tax returns in tabular form as well as on computer micro-data files. Because of changes in tax laws and regulations over the years, the two professors had to make innumerable adjustments to the data. Some of these involved what they referred to as "interpolations," "extrapolations," and "corrections" to the raw IRS data. Their methodology is spelled out in fifteen single-spaced pages (and footnotes) of this ninety-two-page paper and as the authors said, more of the methodology could be provided upon request. Needless to say, this is a very complicated piece of academic research.

But this is the critical point: It's research! As we all know from medical research, sometimes it is right and sometimes it is wrong. For example, remember the debate over caffeine and its effects on the human body…or estrogen? And what about the debates over the use of stents or open heart surgery for opening clogged blood vessels? Research is research, and should be reported as such. Upon reading the Piketty-Saez methodology, I winced when I read part of the methodology relating to correcting the income levels at the tippity-top of the income distribution for capital gains, especially in light of what I had just read in the newspaper.[16] It is one thing to make estimates of the size distribution of income based on a host of assumptions, etc., and have them published in an academic paper, but quite another to have the results of this work published as fact in one of the nation's leading newspapers. It becomes, simply, fuel for the muddle.

One conclusion these economists make in this particular research paper, however, should be mentioned. Their research indicated that the composition of incomes at the top of the income distribution over the 1913-2002 period had changed quite profoundly over the last few decades. It had shifted from income derived from capital, such as dividends and interest, to that of income derived from wages and salaries, or as these authors stated, "…the coupon clipping rentiers have been overtaken by the working rich."[17] To their way of thinking, this was the factor driving income inequality upward—to which I can only say, thank goodness, the rich were at least working!

And a postscript to this discussion involves another piece of research into the upper income strata of our nation. Xavier Gabaix and Augustin Landier, two economists from the New York University's Stern School of Business, undertook an examination into the widely reported explosion in CEO pay.[18] According to their work, the six-fold increase in CEO compensation between 1980 and 2003 was almost totally explained by the roughly six-fold increase in the market capitalization of large corporations. But, of course, this research received less publicity from the mainstream media.

Notes

1.   Ben S. Bernanke, Chairman, Federal Reserve Board, "The Level and Distribution of Economic Well-Being," Before the Greater Omaha Chamber of Commerce, Omaha, Nebraska, Feb. 6, 2007.
2.   Herman P. Miller, "Is the Income Gap Closed? No!" *The New York Times*, (Magazine section), Nov. 11, 1962.
3.   David Brooks, "Dollars and Sense," *The New York Times*, Jan. 26, 2006.

4.   Bernard Goldberg, *Bias: A CBS Insider Exposes How the Media Distort the News* (Washington, DC: Regnery, 2001); and Bernard Goldberg, *Arrogance: Rescuing America From the Media Elite* (New York: Warner Books, 2003). Of course, conservative talk show hosts are frequently attacking the left-leaning print and electronic media on their programs as well.

5.   Ben J. Wattenberg, *The Good News is The Bad News is Wrong* (New York: Simon and Schuster, 1984).

6.   Pew Research Center, "Trends in Political Values and Core Attitudes," Washington, DC, March 22, 2007 (http://www.people-press.org).

7.   Richard Siklos, "Potential Jurors Know Little About Ex-Media Tycoon," *New York Times,* March 15, 2007, p. C2.

8.   Don Imus, "Imus in the Morning," MSNBC, January 5, 2005.

9.   Griffe Witte, "As Income Gap Widens, Uncertainty Spreads," *The Washington Post,* September 20, 2004, pp. A1, A8, and A9.

10.   The "hollowing out" terminology was first used by Frank Levy and Richard J. Murnane in an article reviewing the proliferating research into earnings trends and earnings inequality back in the early 1990s. See "U.S. Earnings Levels and Earnings Inequality: A Review of Recent Trends and Explanations," *Journal of Economic Literature* (September 1992); pp. 1364-1371.

11.   For a comprehensive review of this issue see, Frank Levy, *The New Dollar and Dreams* (New York: Russell Sage Foundation, 1998), Chapter 4, Occupational Change: Can the Economy Still Produce Good Jobs and, If So, Who Gets Them?, pp. 77-125.

12.   See, Paul Ryscavage, Gordon Green, and Edward Welniak, "The Impact of Demographic, Social, and Economic Change on the Distribution of Incomes, in *Studies in the Distribution of Income,* (P60-183) U.S. Bureau of the Census, HHES Division (Washington, DC: USGPO, 1992), pp. 11-26.

13.   *Income, Poverty, and Health Insurance Coverage in the United States: 2004* (P60-229), U.S. Bureau of the Census, HHES Division (Washington, DC: USGPO, August 2005), p. 7.

14.   David Cay Johnston, "Income Gap Is Widening, Data Shows," *The New York Times,* March 29, 2007, pp. C1 and C10.

15.   Thomas Piketty and Emmanuel Saez, "Income Inequality in the United States, 1913-2002," Nov. 2004 (http://elsa.berkeley.edu/~saez/piketty-saezOUP04us.pdf).

16.   *Ibid.*, p. 34.

17.   *Ibid.*, p. 26.

18.   Laura Vanderkam, "Cracking the CEO Pay Puzzle," *The American*, March/April, 2008. See also, Xavier Gabaix and Augustin Landier, "Why Has CEO Pay Increased So Much?" *The Quarterly Journal of Economics,* February 2008, pp. 49-100.

2

The *Reality* of Growing Income Inequality

The rich don't exploit the poor. They just out-compete them.
—David Brooks

Our initial perceptions of income differences probably come to us at a very young age. They did for me. I remember mine from growing up in a New England mill town back in the 1950s.

One of the richest men in town lived up the hill across the street from my family in a yellow, stucco house with a veranda that wrapped half-way around and a fancy brick chimney running up its side. A four-door, tail-finned Cadillac was always parked along its side. He owned the bakery and made all the bread for the town.

We lived in a cream-colored frame house, with a screened-in front porch, and a skinny little chimney. My father was a school superintendent. In our driveway sat a two-door, pea-green Chevrolet. Our neighbors, on our side of the street, were mill foremen, mill workers, and shop owners from town who lived in similar looking houses as mine.

Across the river and the tracks, that ran in back of my house, stood the textile mill. It was the major employer in town. Most of the mill workers and their families lived right next to the mill in Three Rows, in the boxy tenements that were lined up like pieces in a Monopoly game. I figured out at a pretty young age that they weren't as well-off as we were and certainly not as well-off as the baker across the street. But it didn't matter since many of my friends came from there.

So you might say I had some sense, at a very young age, of what the income distribution looked like, especially in my town. But as far as changes in it go—or increasing income inequality, in particular—I'm not so sure.

I remember when the mill closed and moved south in the mid-1950s. It was a big deal and I recall the workers returning home to Three Rows after the "last" second shift. My friends and I knew this wasn't a good thing, but I didn't realize at the time that income inequality in my town was about to grow. Days and months went by and lots of the mill workers were collecting unemployment checks and some were finding jobs in other towns. My father was okay because he was in education, and the baker, well, he began to thrive because he expanded his business to neighboring towns. I figured he was richer than ever. But again, I didn't know what was happening to income inequality. Nobody did.

The point of my little vignette is this: We all come into this world amidst income differences that we eventually come to recognize, but when these differences in incomes of people become larger (or smaller), most Americans don't have a clue as to what is happening to income inequality—*except* when economists measure it.

Measuring Income Inequality

Economists and others interested in the income and wealth differences in society have a variety of methods for measuring these differences, ranging from very simple ones to very complex ones. In the case of income inequality, a couple were mentioned in passing in the previous chapter (e.g., income classes, income shares).

Measurement begins by first defining "income." While to the average Joe in the street this may seem silly, but some economists have struggled with this very subject for a long time. For our purposes, we'll follow the "average Joe's" understanding of income as the money received by persons, families, and households from a variety of sources, like the wages and salaries from jobs, and the dividends, interest, and rent from investments, and the retirement incomes from Social Security, pensions, and annuities that are received over a period of time, such as a year.

Typically, all of this income information for these income recipients is then arranged from those with the lowest incomes to those with the highest. The result is an income distribution. And it is to this that the economists apply their measuring tools. The actual measurement usually involves the lowest and highest parts of the income distribution, but not always. Some of the simplest measurements involve:

- Income classes (e.g., $35,000 to $49,999…$100,000 to $149,999)
- Shares of income received by fractions of the income distribution (e.g., the lowest 20 percent, the top 20 percent, the top 1 percent)
- Income ratios at percentiles of the income distribution (e.g., 90th/10th)

Income classes were used in the *Washington Post* story cited in Chapter 1 so as to define the middle class, and shares of income were used in the *New York Times* article to discuss the nation's rich.

More complex income inequality measures are based on statistical methods and techniques and can be (but not always) summarized in a single statistic. Some of these are:

- The coefficient of variation
- The variance of the natural logarithm of incomes
- Mean logarithmic deviation of incomes
- The Gini index
- The Theil index
- The Atkinson indexes

These measures are seldom reported in the mainstream media because of their technical nature, but they are used extensively in academic *research* as well as by the U.S. Census Bureau and other organizations in their analyses of the nation's income distribution.

The important point is that it is from these income inequality measurements (as well as others) that the mainstream media obtains its information about growing income inequality, or the widening income gap. Without them, and those who make the measurements, the media and, more importantly, their readers, viewers, and listeners wouldn't have a clue of what's going on!

First Signs of Rising Inequality

Because it has been primarily the economists in academia, the government, and other institutions who are interested in tracking the economic well-being of society, it's to them we must look to discover the *true* reality of growing income inequality.

The study of the income distribution has traditionally been confined to the backwaters of serious economic analysis. This humble status existed for many years despite the fact that David Ricardo (1772-1823), one of the elites in the pantheon of economics, believed that understanding the laws determining how a nation's economic output is distributed was one of the central concerns of political economy.[1]

In the first half of the twentieth century, for example, a period of extreme income inequality and one of great economic instability (e.g., the Great Depression), economists were more concerned with issues related to economic growth and the business cycle.

But one illustrious economist of the first half of the last century who concerned himself with income inequality was Simon Kuznets, a Nobel prize winner. Indeed, Kuznets posited a theory concerning what happened to income inequality in a nation whose economic base was changing from agriculture to industry.[2] His theory was that inequality rose when a part of the low-paid agricultural work force began migrating to urban areas for better paying jobs; as the process continued and more and more agricultural workers moved into the industrial work force, inequality would soon stabilize and then decline.

The important point of Kuznets' work is the fact that, although his theory is of questionable validity, his prediction of the inequality trend smacked of reality in those early years of the last century. Income inequality had risen to great heights by the end of the 1930s and then plummeted during the 1940s and 1950s, indeed reaching its lowest point in the mid-1960s. From the end of the nineteenth century to mid-way through the twentieth then, the trend in income inequality could be represented by an inverted "U."

Present day interest in the nation's income gap had its origins in the 1960s, as mentioned earlier (but it took another decade or so to really get rolling). On the one hand this may appear odd, since the nation's income data suggested that income inequality was relatively low during these years as compared to the past. On the other hand, the nation had just passed through some turbulent years when an unpopular war in Vietnam, a festering civil rights movement, and a rambunctious youth cohort tweaked the social conscience of the nation. Issues involving social justice were becoming acutely important.

Economists, especially those in Federal government, had spent much of their time in the 1960s studying the problems of the poor and formulating President Lyndon B. Johnson's War on Poverty. By the early 1970s, however, other economic problems were emerging. After a particularly severe recession in those years, the labor market earnings of workers, along with their productivity, began to falter. Furthermore, inflationary pressures began mounting brought about by increases in food and fuel prices. The attention of economists was now spread across a variety of economic problems, and at its focal point was the functioning of the labor market and workers' earnings.

Among the many economic studies of that period, which focused on the earnings and wages of workers, there was one that, although not directly addressing the problem of slow wage growth, did have important ramifications for how one assessed issues of economic fairness and equity.

The study was conducted by Peter Henle, the former chief economist at the U.S. Bureau of Labor Statistics in 1972, and he examined *earnings inequality* using Census Bureau data for the 1958 to 1970 period.[3] According to his analysis of the earnings distribution over this period, he observed "a slow but persistent trend toward inequality." This might have appeared to be a fairly innocuous finding but it wasn't. In simple terms it meant that earnings were changing at different rates *across* the earnings distribution, that is, some were changing faster than others. This was perhaps the first time in many years that economic outcomes of workers—low wage, medium wage, high wage workers—were being compared across the earnings spectrum.

The finding by Henle caught the eyes of many, including *The New York Times*.[4] It did so not only because of the implicit fairness issue it raised, but because of the analytical sophistication he had brought to his work. To determine whether or not the earnings distribution of men was growing more unequal, he employed as his measures of inequality, the shares of wage and salary earnings received by each quintile (each 20 percent of earners) of the distribution and the "Gini" index of income concentration.[5] These measures had been employed before in analyses of income distributions to determine how concentrated incomes were. However, it was the first time (or if not, the first time in many years) the results of the measurements ended up on the front page of the nation's premier newspaper.

Henle's 1972 inequality analysis of earnings distributions was later updated by himself and Paul Ryscavage in 1980.[6] This analysis found that inequality among male earners had become particularly concentrated in the 1968 to 1973 period. They too had employed the "shares" and Gini index in their analysis. Although this paper did not garner the attention of the national media, it did so in the academic community. Shortly after the appearance of the Henle-Ryscavage study a number of academic economists examined the earnings distributions of workers and their trends—using different data and different techniques—and reached similar conclusions: Inequality was on the rise—the economic lot of some workers was changing faster than for others. The issue of economic fairness and equity had arrived on center stage.

The Drift Towards Growing Income Inequality

Interest in earnings inequality in the early 1980s was further advanced by the severe economic recession that occurred at that time. Economists were now digging deeper into the data from the Census Bureau and elsewhere; they were observing that workers' average earnings, which were barely growing in the 1970s, were now actually in decline. And the decline was most severe for the lowest skilled and poorest trained workers who occupied the lower half of the earnings distribution.

In a popular book at that time, two economists, Barry Bluestone and Bennett Harrison, warned that something dangerous was happening to the industrial structure of the nation's economy—de-industrialization.[7] The implication of their analysis was that the slow growth in wages and the growing wage gap was jeopardizing the economic health of the nation's middle class, so much so, that it was in—a state of decline! The Bluestone-Harrison book and their subsequent work received national media attention and engendered considerable debate during the 1980s. More than any other analysis, theirs had implicitly shifted attention from earnings inequality to income inequality. The notion of economic fairness and equity, introduced onto the national stage via an analysis of worker's earnings distributions, had now spread to the nation's income distribution.

Two developments were sparked by the "declining" middle class issue. First, for economists a "cottage industry" had just been created. And second, a media "feeding frenzy" had just been unleashed. No one could have imagined a more natural symbiosis—one that endures to this very day.

It is not important to recapitulate all of the significant studies and analyses of economic inequality in the United States that were produced over the ensuing decades. Nor is it important to sift through the more salient news stories and media accounts about this nation's income gap. It would be like paddling through the flotsam and jetsam of a WWII naval battle. What is important is to present the basic trends in income inequality since the 1960s as identified by perhaps the most impartial source of such information: the Census Bureau.

Income Inequality According to the Census Bureau

Each year the Census Bureau, through a sample survey of approximately 100,000 household addresses, asks the heads of these households about their previous year's annual income (see Appendix A for a discussion). From these data, Census Bureau analysts compute income statistics reflecting the incomes of all households in the country. Among the many statistics they compute, including the nation's poverty rate, are a variety of income inequality measures, some of which were identified earlier in the chapter. The trend lines in Figure 2.1 represent five unique measures of income inequality over the 1967 to 2006 period.[8]

Figure 2.1
Income Inequality Indexes
1967 to 2006

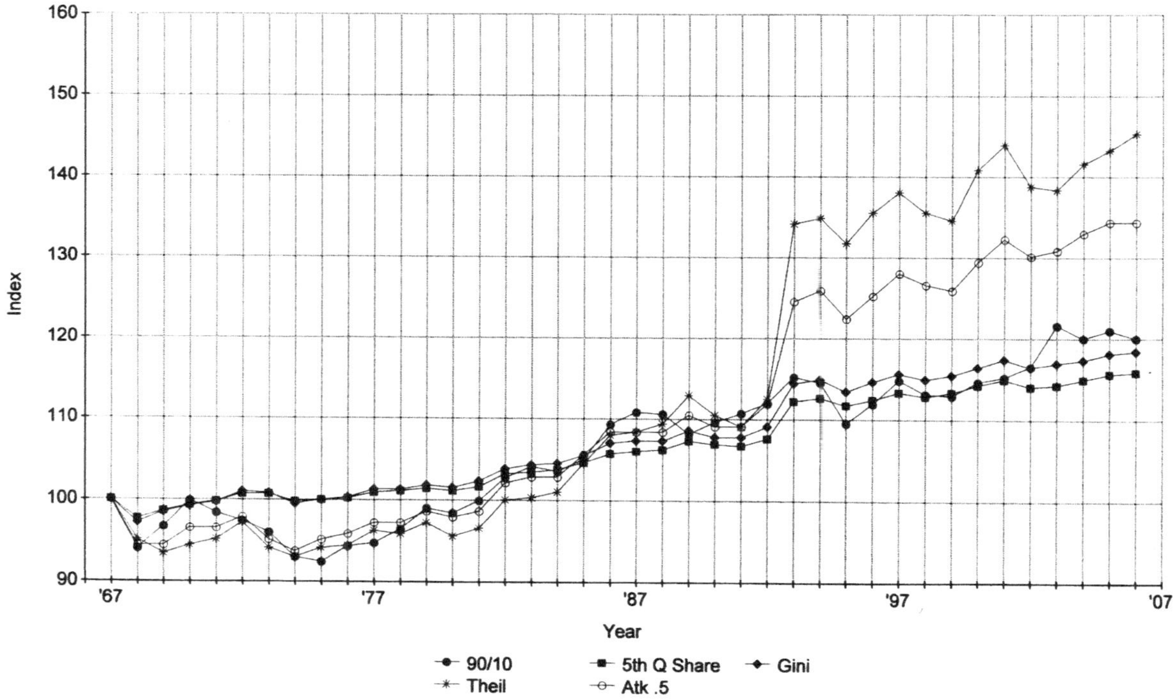

Although the Federal government has an "official" unemployment rate and "official" inflation rate and an "official" economic growth rate, it does not have an "official" income inequality measure. So the Census Bureau provides a number of different measures of income inequality—some quite simple, others quite sophisticated. Changes over the past years in some of these measures are shown in the figure.

Each of the measures has a unique metric, that is, the statistics are not easily compared because they are calculated differently. But this isn't important because what is of interest are the rates of change in each measure across this thirty-nine-year period. Consequently each measure—the 90th/10th income percentile ratio, the highest income quintile share, the Gini index, the Theil index, and the Atkinson (.50) index—has been indexed so that their values in 1967 are all equivalent to 100.0. Each year's subsequent value, therefore, has been made "relative" to the value in 1967 in the form of an index, in other words, a percentage change in each inequality measure since 1967.

For all the mainstream media's attention to the income gap in recent years, rarely do they provide a statistical measure of it—and for a very good reason. There are so many measures of income inequality. In addition, one never hears about how fast inequality has been rising in recent years—and this too is because there are so many measures. For example, of all the five measures presented in Figure 2.1, the Theil index registers the fastest growth over the 1967 to 2006 period (around 45 percent) while the highest income quintile share registers the slowest (around 15 percent). So, at best, these measures tell us that income inequality has risen in the second half of the 20th century and into the 21st, but how fast it has been rising depends on the measure being examined.

The Theil, Gini, and Atkinson indexes of income inequality in the figure are based on complicated calculations and summarize inequality in the entire income distribution. The 90th/10th percentile income ratio and the highest income quintile share involve simpler calculations and reflect measurements at specific points and areas of the income distribution. But they all, together, provide us with some insights into the reality of growing income inequality in the 1967 to 2006 period—and it is not necessary to understand how each of these measures are calculated.

First, notice that all of them register very little increase in the 1967 to 1977 period, but then they drift slowly upward throughout the 1980s. These later years, of course, represent the time when economists were expanding their analyses of workers' earnings distributions to now include the incomes of families and households. The second point to notice is that at the end of the 1980s and into the early 1990s, the upward drift slowed and stabilized. This, of course, was the period leading up to the economic recession of 1990 and 1991.

The third, and most perplexing part of the figure to explain, at least on first glance, is the trend in inequality between the early 1990s and 2006. The sudden surge in inequality between 1992 and 1993 is part real and part synthetic.[9] Some of the increase in income inequality was simply due to the recovery from the economic recession (which affected a large proportion of middle to upper income families) and methodological changes in the way income data were collected by the Census Bureau. Obviously, the Theil and Atkinson indexes were greatly affected. Nevertheless, it would appear that inequality continued to *gradually* move upward after this, especially according to the Theil and Atkinson measure. In the early years of the new century, three out of the five measures appeared to lose their upward momentum, perhaps reflecting the downturn in the economy.

Comparing this rather clinical examination of inequality in the income distribution to what Americans have been told via the mainstream media should be eye-opening. While the simple fact that the nation's income distribution has become more dispersed in the last few decades cannot be disputed, the extent and degree of the dispersion is open to conjecture.

Have we become a nation of *only* rich and poor people? Has the middle class hollowed out? Are the ranks of the poor swelling with welfare Moms and immigrant families crushed by our free-market system? The Census Bureau data help in answering these questions.

Inside the Income Distribution

The Census Bureau also provides statistics that get us inside the nation's income distribution, much like the 90th/10th percentile income ratio and the amount of income received by the richest 20 percent of households (i.e., the highest income quintile share). What the statistics about to be presented show is *where* inside the distribution did the widening, or movement towards inequality, take place during the 1967 to 2006 period. These statistics are readily available and appear in Census Bureau publications.

Figure 2.2 presents three additional income percentile ratios for the 1967 to 2006 period. These are the 95th/50th, 80th/50th, and 20th/50th income percentile ratios.[10] Unlike the 90th/10th income percentile ratio used in Figure 2.1, these ratios have not been indexed and reflect their nominal values in each year. In other words, with these ratios one can

Figure 2.2
Income Ratios–Poverty Rate
1967 to 2006

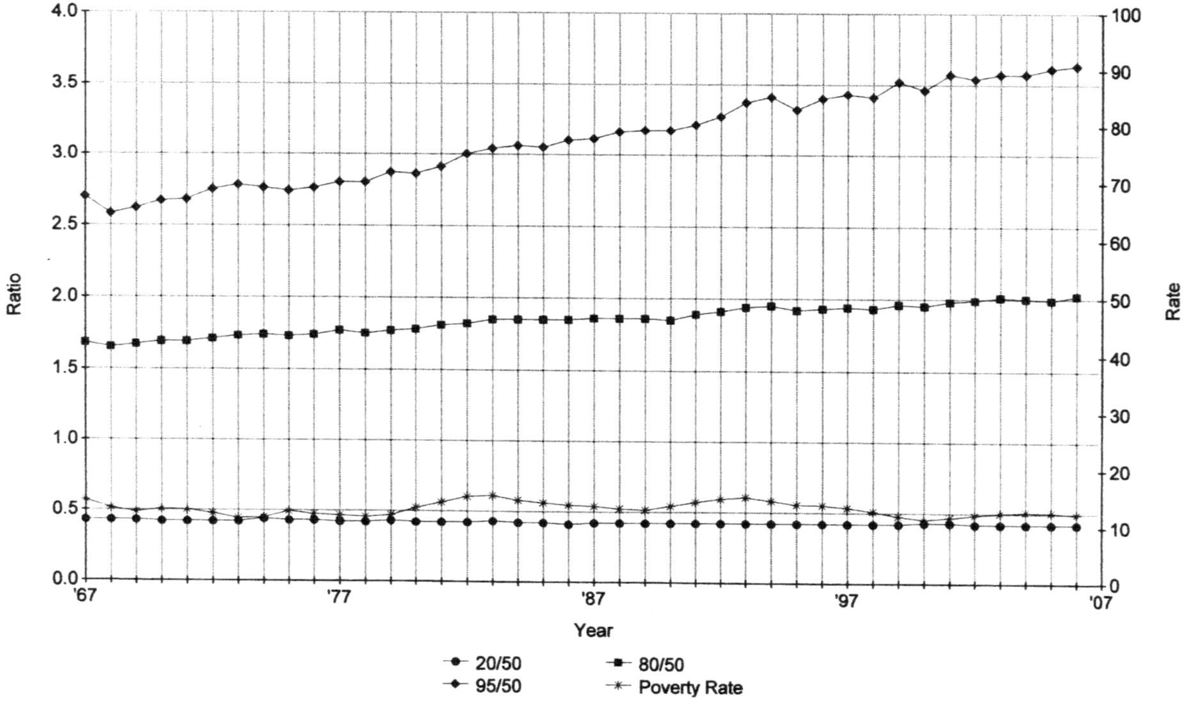

see where the income distribution was expanding relative to the median household income of the distribution, or the income at the 50th percentile.

The reality of growing income inequality can be quickly observed from the figure. The 20th/50th income percentile ratio varied only slightly in a narrow range from .41 to .44 over the entire 39 years. This means, of course, the household income of households with the median income and the income at the 20th percentile rose similarly over this period—roughly 30 percent in inflation adjusted dollars.[11] In contrast, both the 95th/50th and 80th/50th ratios increased, the former from 2.70 to 3.63, and the latter from 1.68 to 2.02. This reflects faster rising incomes at the 95th percentile and at the 80th percentile, respectively, than at the median. In the former case income had increased by 78 percent and in the latter by 59 percent. The inequality in the income distribution, therefore, was being caused by households whose annual incomes were above the median income of all households and rising faster than those at the median. It was not due to a collapse of middle class incomes, or the "hollowing out" of the income distribution, nor by the growth of households at the lower end of the income distribution. The popular nickname for what American society had become—a "have and have not" nation—was hyperbole.

Another revealing statistic about the reality of growing income inequality in the country is also provided by the Census Bureau—the poverty rate.[12] This statistic appears in Figure 2.2 as well. As is shown there, the incidence of poverty over the 1967 to 2006 period has varied within a narrow range of from 11.1 to 15.2 percent with the highest rates associated with economic recessions. (One could have assumed as much from the apparent stable relationship exhibited in the 20th/50th income percentile ratio as shown in the figure.) After a short recession in the opening years of this century, the poverty rate in 2006 was 12.3 percent and in 1967 it was 14.2 percent. The traditional view that a widening income gap meant "the rich were becoming more numerous at the same time the poverty rate was increasing" was another myth. Nevertheless, the fact remains, millions of Americans—36 million of them in 2006—lived in poverty.

Pausing for Pareto...and the Poor

This *reality* of growing income inequality flies in the face of what many "liberal-minded" economists, politicians, media outlets, and ordinary citizens believe about what happened to this country's income distribution over recent years. Economists will point to the simplicity of this analysis; the liberal politicians will call it hard-hearted, right wing rhetoric; the media will ignore it; and left-leaning, egalitarian-minded citizens will point to the gated communities and tax breaks for the rich. So be it, but the facts are there.

And how does one evaluate the implications of these facts? How does one arrive at a moral or ethical assessment of these income inequality trends over the last three or four decades? We certainly know what the mainstream media has come to believe, as well as those on the political left. But setting aside their views, what can you make of these changes in the annual household incomes of Americans?

Most economists tend to shy away from moral judgments, but rather seek to understand the "hows and whys" of an economy's operation. Nevertheless, some economists over time have attempted to develop guidelines, or criterion, for assessing economic change and its consequence for the economic welfare of society.[13] Among these was Vilfredo Pareto (1848-1923), an Italian mathematician and economist, whose work has been highly regarded in this domain.

Pareto's criterion for evaluating economic change has been stated in various ways but basically it amounts to this: An economic change is *good* if it at least makes someone better off without making anyone worse off. If we assume that the economic policies put into place by our government over the last several decades have affected the economy and therefore the people who are a part of it, we could use the Pareto criterion to evaluate the consequences of these policies. And one of the obvious pieces of evidence about the economic consequences of these policies are the incomes of American families and households.

The Census Bureau data in Table 2.1 are the mean (average) annual incomes (in 2006 dollars) of households in the five quintiles of the income distribution for 1967 and 2006, and the percent change in those incomes over this period.[14] As the data show, real average household income rose fastest in the highest income quintile—83 percent—followed by a real income increase of almost 50 percent in the fourth income quintile. This is the fact that the elite media frequently report, that all of the economic rewards in recent years have been reaped by those in the upper part of the income distribution. But, of course, that was not the case.

As is also shown in the table, average incomes increased in all the lower quintiles as well. Even for the lowest quintile, average real income rose by 38 percent, while somewhat lower increases were recorded in the second (26 percent) and third quintiles (32 percent). Overall household income increased by 62 percent in inflation adjusted dollars in the 1967-

Table 2.1
Average Annual Income (in 2006 dollars) of Households by
Quintiles of the Income Distribution, 1967 and 2006

Quintile	2006	1967	Percent change
All Quintiles	$66,570	$41,212	61.5
Lowest	11,352	8,252	37.6
2nd	28,777	22,866	25.9
3rd	48,223	36,509	32.1
4th	76,329	51,081	49.4
Highest	168,170	91,926	82.9

Source: U.S. Census Bureau

2006 period. According to the Pareto criterion, therefore, since everyone's economic situations improved over the last three or four decades the economic policies of the nation produced a "Pareto improvement" for our society.

But the number of economists subscribing to the Pareto guideline is hard to know. One well-known economist, however, who does believe in the Pareto criterion is Martin Feldstein, a former chairman of the White House's Council of Economic Advisers and a Harvard University professor. In 1998 at a Federal Reserve Bank of Kansas City symposium on income inequality he suggested that the growth in income inequality (brought on by faster growing incomes in the upper half of the income distribution) was a "good thing" and not a "bad thing" as so frequently heard in the media and by others.[15] He said:

> I reject such arguments and stick to the basic interpretation of the Pareto principle that if the material well-being of some individuals increases with no decreases in the well-being of others, that is a good thing even if it implies an increase in measured inequality.[16]

He went on to suggest that when one examines the more rapid growth among the top income households one sees individuals with the following traits and characteristics: high productivity, entrepreneurial spirit, willingness to work hard and long hours, and the ability to take advantage of low capital costs (interest rates). He contends that simply because others in society were not able to avail themselves of such traits and characteristics are not grounds for viewing growing income inequality as "so unlovely."

Clearly, rising inequality would be another matter if society's economic well-being was behaving like a children's seesaw, that is, with real average incomes actually decreasing in the lower quintiles and increasing in the upper quintiles. But that was not the case. The fact that the incidence of poverty in the United States changed relatively little over the last several decades is further evidence of the general rise in real household incomes for everyone. Unfortunately, for some the income rise was insufficient to lift their households out of poverty. Indeed, Feldstein acknowledged that the real problem in the nation was not growing inequality of incomes but the persistency of poverty. So, the Pareto criterion is a useful tool in assessing *changes* in the distribution of income over time, but it is not very helpful when looking at the distribution at a point in time—and the sticking point, of course, is poverty.

Poverty and its causes has received considerable attention in this nation for many, many years, and will continue to do so until everyone can agree that it has been eliminated. The political right has their views on how to attack it and the political left has theirs—and both have had their opportunities to do something about it, but with varying degrees of success. In the earlier years of our country's history, economic growth and opportunities appeared to be the best prescription for reducing poverty. But ever since the late 1960s and early 1970s, the measured rate of poverty, as mentioned above, has only varied within a narrow range in the low teens—despite a growing economy.

Is this the best our economic system can do? Are we destined to always have a certain proportion of the population living below a "poverty line" however it is defined? If the answers to these questions are yes, then what are our obligations to the poor to improve their economic lot in life so they can be referred to as "nonpoor?" If the answers are no, then how do we change the things we have tried to reduce poverty so as to make them *more* successful so it can be eliminated?

Answers to these questions, of course, only sink us deeper into these complex topics of ethics, morality, and justice—and what we believe as Americans.

What's Fair Anyway?

Arguing about fairness is a great American pastime and probably anywhere in the world where there are at least two people. This is no doubt true whatever kind of fairness we're talking about, whether it is in the political arena or academic arena or sports arena or economic arena. And it is this latter kind of fairness—economic fairness—that we are interested in.

Let me be up front about this right away. Even if your household income rises by 100 percent in one year, if your income still falls below the poverty line you are still poor. When incomes are not adequate according to socially agreed upon standards, overall economic welfare is diminished and it is not at the level it should be. At the heart of the matter is basic human decency and human justice.

Economic fairness has been a topic of concern for man down through the ages as he struggled with organizing his society. Aristotle mused over it. It was thought of in the broad context of justice, and in this specific case as, "distributive justice." How should the material necessities of life be allocated? For Aristotle, a fair allocation should be based on merit because human beings are unequal. Consequently, inequality would be the natural state of the distribution and it would be fair.

Skipping across two millenniums of thought on this topic can be easily justified because we know that all the moral teachings and philosophical thought that has gone into this topic has undergone the human filtration and distillation process resulting in what today could be called mankind's "bi-polar approach" for achieving economic fairness. This bi-polar approach has resulted in two unique distributive systems whose fairness principles can be summarized in the following two phrases:

- To each according to what he and the instruments he owns produces and;
- from each according to his ability, to each according to his needs.

The first phrase is attributed to Milton Friedman.[17] It, of course, reflects the distributional principle in a free market, capitalistic society, such as the United States. It is rooted in both the principles of freedom and private property, and all the individual rights that attend to them. Its moral basis can be found in Christian scripture.[18] The second phrase is attributed to Karl Marx.[19] Its distributional principle is from the communist tradition, and reflective of a communistic society such as present day Cuba. It to, of course, has a religious basis.[20]

This bi-polar approach to economic fairness, of course, represents the extremes of a range of distributive systems around the world. When media reports speak about the nations of Western Europe representing "welfare states" they are suggesting that their distributive systems are more reflective—at least in spirit—of the second phrase than the first. Indeed, one religious thinker on this subject has identified five economic systems in which the manner of distribution and allocation of resources differs.[21] These are:

- Marxism
- Social Market Capitalism
- Democratic Socialism
- Economic Conservationism
- Laissez Faire Capitalism

According to this thinker, the two systems at the extremes have flaws and virtues, while the middle three systems take the best from the extremes without being burdened by the flaws. The middle three systems can be committed to democracy and human rights and bear allegiance to Christian virtues. Their range of differences are based on the extent "…to which we must hitch the wagon of economics to incentives based upon selfishness in order to get the work done and upon the extent to which we must base economic policy upon the limits of earth."[22]

Each of these five systems has identifiable rules and precepts by which economic activity and distribution is arranged in society. In other words, the people who live in these societies are aware of (or are suppose to be) the way their particular distributive system operates. Nevertheless, given the basic nature of man, dissatisfaction with a particular system is inevitable (i.e., It's not fair!).

In our own country, for example, public discourse is loaded with debate about the fairness of our economic system (which most would agree is closer to resembling laissez faire capitalism than democratic socialism and, of course, Marxism). This debate is not only found in the media but in the lofty reaches of academia. The late John Rawls, a Harvard professor, set forth in his book, *A Theory of Justice* (as well as other writings), a principle of distributive justice that has spawned much of this debate.[23] Rawls crafted his principle to fit, what he perceived to be, the American distributive system. His principle incorporates the equal rights and opportunities of all people and acknowledges the existence of social and economic inequalities caused by the innate differences in human beings. *But* these inequalities, Rawls prescribes, must eventually benefit those at the bottom of the economic ladder. This is to say that the benefit of the inequalities should accrue to the poor (perhaps, through an "incentive" effect); this can be the only justification in a society for economic inequality.

Rawls's theory of justice has a strong moral core, consistent with the precepts of major religions that emphasize social justice and caring for society's poor. Despite its altruistic appeal, it has been criticized for its "controlling" implications. That is, his principle places the poor and downtrodden at the mercy of those who have been economically successful. And another more cold-hearted and straight-forward criticism is that Rawls's principle is inconsistent with an economic system built upon merit (like ours) in which one's share of society's output is thought to be related to one's contribution to it.

At the other end of the political-economic spectrum there is the case of the Peoples' Republic of China, a nation born in the mid-twentieth century and organized on the principles of Marxism. Over the decades, restrictions on economic freedoms, markets, and private property have slowly been loosened. By the beginning of the twenty-first century, the economic power of the world's most populous nation was being felt in its neighboring countries as well as the Western world. These changes did not come about without debate inside China over economic fairness and how the Chinese nation could improve its economic life. And clearly, the Chinese have these debates at various levels as well—from the governmental compounds of Beijing to the streets of Shanghai.

The central issue in their debate is how free should markets become. This debate too has a fundamentally moral overtone to it that deals with basic human rights and liberties. Those who oppose this drift towards greater economic freedoms are concerned with the growing divide between rural and urban China (and economic inequalities) and the erosion of basic Marxist teachings.

Obviously, the answer to the question raised at the beginning of this section depends on one's value system and the mores of one's society. The search for economic fairness proceeds on various tracks and according to certain core beliefs. The important point to remember is that what everyone is seeking is fairness—and justice—which is consistent with the rules. The eternal problem, of course, is that rules change, and perhaps this is simply a characteristic of the human condition.

Notes

1.   David Ricardo, *The Principles of Political Economy and Taxation*, No. 590 of Everyman's Library, edited by Ernest Rhys, (London: J.M Dent & Sons Limited, 1911), in the Original Preface of 1817.

2.   Simon Kuznets, *Shares of Upper Income Groups in Income and Savings* (New York: National Bureau of Economic Research, 1953). The study of our country's income distribution in the first half of the twentieth century has mushroomed

in recent years, presumably in response to public awareness over the widening income gap in the second half of that century.

3.   Peter Henle, "Exploring the Distribution of Earned Income," *Monthly Labor Review*, December, 1972, pp. 16-27.

4.   Philip Shabecoff, "Study Finds Incomes More Unequal," *The New York Times*, December 27, 1972, p. 1 and p. 22.

5.   The Gini index of income concentration was developed by the Italian mathematician Corrado Gini (1884-1965) and because it is used and referred to extensively in this book, a brief description of it is provided in Appendix A.

6.   Peter Henle and Paul Ryscavage, "The Distribution of Earned Income Among Men and Women, 1958-77," *Monthly Labor Review*, April, 1980, pp. 3-10.

7.   Barry Bluestone and Bennett Harrison, *The Deindustrialization of America* (New York: Basic Books, 1982).

8.   *Income, Poverty, and Health Insurance Coverage in the United States: 2006*, (P60-233), U.S. Bureau of the Census, HHES Division (Washington, DC: USGPO, August 2007), Table A-3, pp. 38-39.

9.   See Paul Ryscavage, "A Surge in Growing Inequality?" *Monthly Labor Review*, August, 1995, pp. 51-61.

10.   *Income, Poverty, and Health Insurance Coverage in the United States: 2006*, (P60-233), U.S. Bureau of the Census, Table A-3, pp. 38-39.

11.   Usage of terms such as real, constant dollars, inflation adjusted dollars, or, in 2004 dollars (etc.), indicate that wages, earnings, incomes, or wealth and their trends have been adjusted for inflation. Terms such as nominal or current dollars indicate that they have not been adjusted for inflation.

12.   *Income, Poverty, and Health Insurance Coverage in the United States: 2006* (P60-233), U.S. Bureau of the Census, Table B-1, p. 44.

13.   Indeed, a small but distinct branch of economics is devoted to this task, and appropriately enough, is called welfare economics.

14.   *Income, Poverty, and Health Insurance in the United States: 2006* (P60-233), U.S. Bureau of the Census, Table A-3, pp. 38-39.

15.   Martin Feldstein, "Overview," *Symposium Proceedings: Income Inequality Issues and Policy Options*, A symposium sponsored by the Federal Reserve Bank of Kansas City, Jackson Hole, Wyoming, August 27-29, 1998 (Kansas City: Federal Reserve Bank of Kansas City, 1998), pp. 357-367.

16.   *Ibid.*, p. 358.

17.   Milton Friedman, *Capitalism and Freedom* (Chicago: The University of Chicago Press, 1962), pp. 161-162.

18.   See New Testament, Thessalonians, Bk. 2 3:10, "...if anyone was unwilling to work, neither should that one eat." *The New American Bible,* The Second Letter to the Thessalonians (Nashville: Catholic Bible Press, 1987), Ch. 3, p. 1358.

19.   This was one of the statements made by Karl Marx in his critical review of the Gotha Programme, a proclamation of the German Workers' Party in the late nineteenth century. See Karl Marx's, *Critique of the Gotha Programmme*, Marginal Notes to the Programme of the German Workers' Party, May 5, 1875.

20.   See New Testament, Acts 4:35, "...and they were distributed to each according to need." *The New American Bible*, Acts, Ch. 4, p. 1228.

21.   J. Phillip Wogaman, *The Great Economic Debate: An Ethical Analysis*, (Philadelphia: The Westminster Press, 1977).

22.   *Ibid.*, p. 156.

23.   John Rawls, *A Theory of Justice* (Cambridge: Harvard University Press, 1971).

3

Understanding Economic Fairness Today

Each man has an equal right to freedom. This is an important and fundamental right precisely because men are different, because one man will want to do different things with his freedom than another, and in the process can contribute more than another to the general culture of the society in which many men live.
—Milton Friedman

Americans don't walk around with a rule book of economic "rights and wrongs" in their hands. What we do have, however, is some sense of how economic life operates in this country and some notions of what is fair and not fair. This sense of economic fairness is derived, for the most part, from the teachings of our religions, the laws governing economic activity, and the general mores of our society.

These beliefs and feelings of Americans about economic fairness, however, are not immutable. Indeed, they have been continually shaped and reshaped, like sand dunes in a desert. Simply consider the changes that have occurred in the economic treatment of women and blacks in the labor market and the host of laws that protect consumers today compared to years ago. In other words, what we consider as fair or unfair today may be just the opposite in the years ahead.

Over the past several decades our sense of economic fairness in this country has been challenged. This is, of course, nothing new. Challenges in the past have occurred in the nation's history—some have been successful and some haven't. The present day challenge began subliminally at a time of major social, economic, and demographic changes in the 1960s, and it has had a profound impact on the national psyche. Like a sticky syrup that seeped into so much of the nation's social fabric, this challenge continues to be in evidence today in various organizations and political groups. But, in many ways, this challenge has helped us *rethink* the economic events that have cascaded down upon us as we moved deeper into the new millennium.

The Three Pillars of Economic Fairness

The conceptual underpinnings of economic fairness, as it is understood today in the United States, rest upon three pillars: exchange, self-interest and competition, and the Golden Rule. To place the present challenge to economic fairness in perspective, it is instructive to examine these basic building blocks of economic fairness in our nation.

At the heart of economic fairness, of course, lies the process of exchange. By definition, at least two individuals or parties are involved and the subject of the exchange (e.g., labor, commodities, services, money). When an exchange is consummated there is the presumption that what has been exchanged are of equal values, that is, one hour of labor is worth a $10 wage, a newly purchased car is worth the $20,000 on the price tag, and a haircut is worth the $16 barber's fee. In other words, a symmetry of values has been reached in the exchange.

Each party involved in the exchange, of course, considers themselves to have benefited. The employer bought an hour's worth of labor to do some task in his business and the employee received $10 to do with what he or she wishes. Both would not have entered the exchange unless each saw some benefit from it, or in other words, the exchange was in their self-interest. The value of the good or service involved in the exchange, however, is determined by its scarcity and desirability, or supply and demand. Both parties to the exchange assess their needs (and benefits) of the good or service in relation to its supply and demand.

As we all know, even though an exchange has taken place between two parties, one of the parties (or even both) may be unhappy. "I got taken," "I've been robbed," are only a few of the many epithets that have emerged from exchanges. In such instances, of course, fairness is called into question and an *asymmetry* of values has presumably resulted. Such asymmetries sometimes are not even acknowledged but other times they lead to actions in which an effort is made to produce symmetry (e.g., by a law suit, court injunction or decision, legislation).

Behind all economic exchanges in a free market economy are the forces driving the process—self-interest and competition. As shunned as these ideas are in some quarters of contemporary America (about which more will be said), they still represent the motivational factors in an economic exchange. These are the behaviors behind the "invisible hand" of the classical economist, Adam Smith.[1] It was Adam Smith who in the eighteenth century penetrated the workings of England's economic system and laid bare this fundamental economic fact of human life:

It is not from the benevolence of the butcher, the brewer, or the baker, that we expect our dinner, but from their regard to their own interest.[2]

Much of our understanding of the free market system is a result of his thinking.

Self-interest is a very important motivator in our economic lives. Without it our economic welfare would run amuck since we enter economic exchanges in order to benefit from them. My $16 haircut will, hopefully, make me look socially respectable or provide me with some other personal return. In the parlance of the business world, self-interest translates into the profit motive and behaviors designed to maximize profits, whether they be increasing or decreasing prices, hiring or firing workers, or spending more or less money on advertising.

As a consequence of everyone behaving in his or her own self-interest, of course, competition occurs. Workers compete with one another for the highest paying jobs, businesses compete with one another for markets and market share, and consumers compete with one another for the best prices for goods and services. Out of this self-interest and competition comes a free market economy in which the goods and services that consumers want are produced by the workers who are best qualified to do the work, in the businesses that can produce the goods and services at the lowest cost—at least according to Adam Smith. From man's basic instincts, therefore, comes a self-regulating economic system.

But our economic lives, while guided by self-interest and competition, are acted out alongside other aspects of our lives, most importantly our ethical principles and precepts. Philosophers have long thought about the standards of human conduct, or the moral code by which man will live out his life with his fellow man. From Plato to Sartre, they have pondered over the question of goodness in an ever changing world. Many philosophies have been established down through the centuries, only to be eventually forgotten as humankind evolved, or only to be molded or changed into variants of the original thought.

In much of what we commonly refer to as the West, the Christian and Jewish religions have provided us with the guidelines for moral conduct over the last two millenniums or so. From the theologies of both have come what most of us have learned at a young age—the "Golden Rule." Although it has been stated in a variety of ways, it amounts to this: *Treat others as you would like to be treated.* This is a powerful rule and beautiful rule. It is powerful because it can be applied to all aspects of human behavior; it is beautiful because of its implicit symmetry. The application of the Golden Rule in the economic world, specifically the process of exchange, requires that exchanges be of equal value. Indeed, it commands economic fairness.

Is This Class Warfare?

The present day challenge to our society's sense of economic fairness has been manifested in an attack on one of the three pillars of economic fairness—the pillar of self-interest and competition. The charge is made that such behaviors, in the latter part of the twentieth century, grew wild and, in the context of a free market place, produced injustices for segments of our society (indeed, this is a charge leveled at the world's free market system and globalization). The challengers cry out, "Winning is *not* everything!" as their assault on self-interest; and, "Level the playing field!" as their assault on competition.

An outcome of egregious economic unfairness in a society, of course, results in social instability—or revolution—as was the case of the French, Russian, and Cuban revolutions. Socio-economic classes become pitted against one another. In Marxist terms, class warfare was the result.

America does not have a formal class system—at least nothing resembling, for example, that which existed in England or France in previous centuries, or heaven forbid, the class, or caste, system of India. Indeed, America has often prided itself as a "classless" society. What it does have, however, are indistinct "strata" that run through its society like a cross-section of pre-historic earth. And these strata continue to grow more indistinct as the nation evolves and grows older. Nevertheless, some sense of class-consciousness, or class awareness, does exist in our society.

Class differences are apparent everyday and everywhere. Whether we shop downtown on Main Street or out at the mall, whether we watch the CBS Evening News or the Local News on WJWJ, or whether we serve our community when called for jury duty or go to our polling place for an election, class differences are readily apparent to us all. It doesn't matter whether the differences are defined on the basis of wealth, income, wages, education, residence, race, ethnicity, or whatever, it's possible to place the individuals we observe (and ourselves) into the lower, middle, or upper class, and very often, to refine these groups into sub-groups, like the homeless, the working class, or the upper crust. Given this class consciousness on the part of Americans, it is no wonder that the subject of class and class warfare can "pick up our ears" from time-to-time.[3]

Our "Fuzzy" Class System

The existence of social classes in human societies represents man's attempt to make order out of disorder. Once the matter of human survival had been achieved to a satisfactory degree, the next step was to make it more efficient and successful. "Organization" was the answer. Given human differences and capabilities, people eventually sorted themselves (or were sorted) into groups that specialized in tasks associated with the production process.

The specialization of production tasks, whether along the lines of physical or mental ability, economic or political power, spiritual or religious authority, or whatever, has dominated the history of man and resulted in unique groupings of people. Moreover, the economic rewards accruing to these groups have historically been distributed unevenly. Hence, the building blocks for social stratification, or classes, arose from the basic nature of man's existence.

Social stratification, or class systems, is a well-studied subject with plentiful theories and explanations for why class structures have come about, what they look like, how they are changing, and (more alarming), their moral implications. For example, the explanation provided above may be considered Marxian in nature because of its economic orientation, but other explanations, like that of the famous sociologist Max Weber, incorporate noneconomic elements as well.[4] The point is this, one can argue and debate a particular class structure or social stratification system, but, by itself, it doesn't address the fundamental issue of economic fairness unless the moral issues of the day are considered.

Identifying classes in this country, nevertheless, has been a cottage industry for sociologists over the years. One example of such an exercise is shown below. It shows the approximate proportions of our population, according to this particular sociologist, falling into different classes as of the second half of the twentieth century.[5]

Class	Percent
Total	100.0
Upper class	1 to 3
Upper-middle class	10 to 15
Lower-middle class	30 to 35
Working class	40 to 45
Lower class	20 to 25

The designations are straightforward and the proportions and descriptions of each class probably conform to the average person's conception of our country's class structure. The upper class is minute according to this sociologist—1 to 3 percent—and it is made up of people who primarily had inherited their wealth. The upper-middle class represents from 10 to 15 percent of the population and is composed of highly successful doctors and lawyers, as well as highly paid CEOs and business executives. The lower-middle class—30 to 35 percent of the population—is made up also of professional people (but of somewhat lesser status), and is not as well off economically or as well educated as those in the class above them. The working class accounts for 40 to 45 percent of the population (the largest single segment) and consists of the traditional blue-collar workers in skilled and unskilled jobs, but also those who work in relatively low-paying service jobs. The lower class account for 20 to 25 percent of the population and represent the nation's poor and near poor. Included here would be the homeless and underclass that hover near society's subsistence level.

Certainly, this class structure, while conforming to the average man's conception, could be quibbled with because of its precision. For example, many political liberals would suggest that the size of the upper class and lower class are greatly underestimated. Political conservatives, on the other hand, would probably take issue with the estimate of the size of the lower class suggesting it is vastly overestimated. Nevertheless, this depiction is one sociologist's conception of the class structure in this country and it represents the kind of playing field on which perceptions of economic fairness are formed.

Class Struggle?

Class struggle, of course, is closely associated with the economic theory of Karl Marx and how, under the economic system of capitalism, capitalists exploit the proletariat. Marx believed that capitalism was eventually doomed and the proletariat would take over, but only after a long struggle between these two classes. Marx's many predictions, including this one of course, have not come true. Revolutions of the "proletariat" have not taken place in most modern nations of the world, class polarization has not occurred, and capitalism has not collapsed.[6] Nevertheless, Marxist thought—especially that concerning class struggle in capitalist societies—continues to influence much political and social discourse to this very day.

Over the past century, instances of class struggle in our society would be difficult to identify, especially if one's definition of "struggle" meant a protracted period of violence. One could point to the civil rights riots of the 1960s as well as certain labor disturbances that have punctuated the history of the American labor movement, especially those in the 1930s.[7] Indeed, some observers would suggest that these were decades when the nation was on the verge of revolution. But even that social unrest never really reached the "pitchfork-brigades" and "barricades-in-the-streets" level that most people associate with the working class revolts occurring in France in the eighteenth and nineteenth centuries when governments toppled.

What has taken place in this country have been periods of heightened class tension, not class struggle. These periods of unease between the classes (as well as racial, ethnic, and social groups) have arisen—as in the 1930s and 1960s—not only because of economic reasons but because of a combination of social, political, and cultural reasons. Certainly, the tension of the 1930s (when income inequality was at its highest in the century) was due more to economic factors then the tension of the 1960s (when inequality was at its lowest point of the century), which was due more to social and political reasons.

Class tension, of course, is a part of a healthy and normal society in a democratic nation because it provides evidence of a dynamic, pulsating society as opposed to an apathetic and lethargic one. Presumably, in a fair and representative forum of a society, grievances can be adjudicated and corrective measures taken. Class tensions will, therefore, be relaxed and social harmony restored. What is always subject to dispute, however, is whether or not the grievances have been addressed adequately, or for that matter, at all.

Despite the news of the widening income gap in the last decades of the twentieth century, class tension in this country has been moribund. There have been no riots in the streets, no periods of prolonged labor disputes, and no standoffs with groups proclaiming social anarchy that would qualify as having threatened the nation's social stability. But because the news of a widening income gap was spread to a socially and economically diverse society, class-consciousness and class awareness was tweaked. The result, unfortunately, was a rekindling of a *class bias* in isolated pockets of the nation's lower and middle classes directed at the rich.

From Class Consciousness...to Class Bias!

One of the most remarkable social developments in the last few decades has been the reappearance of class bias. It is remarkable because it occurred over a period of time when our society was focused on ridding itself (or trying to) of biases of all kinds—racial, gender, sexual, to name but a few. Simply consider the change that has occurred between the 1970s and 1990s in our speech patterns regarding race, gender, and issues involving gays and lesbians. Beginning for the most part in the 1960s, much of society was preoccupied with eliminating perceived injustices and biases involving race, gender, and sexual preference.

Class bias represents a manner of thinking that inhibits or prevents an objective and impartial perception of a particular social class. While class bias can appear in all classes, in recent years, it has been particularly evident in the feelings and attitudes of some members of the middle and lower classes toward the rich.[8] One can often see and hear these expressions of bias in letters to the editors and remarks on television and over the airwaves. Such people believe the rich have become too rich because of their greed and unfair economic pursuits. Indeed, in some circles, "bashing the rich" has become *derigueur.*

This particular class bias has been fueled by economic events and the manner in which the media have reported such events. Obviously, the increase in income inequality has been the paramount news event. But other events, such as the corporate scandals and the "fairness" debate over President Bush's tax cuts, for example, have often been reported in a way that could be only interpreted as "the rich are running away with the store." Such rhetoric has simply energized the class-consciousness of those members of the middle and lower class with a predisposition to doubt the economic motives of the rich and wealthy.[9]

The result is a class bias, which distorts perceptions of economic fairness. Not only do attitudes and feelings become shrouded in an ethical fog, but economic behavior is apt to be affected by the bias. Everyone has heard the expression, "Let's soak 'em!"

Class bias against the rich is not exactly a new social development. Indeed, an undercurrent of class bias toward the rich has run quietly through the lower class and working class during the first half of the last century because it was an aspect of class consciousness. As George Gilder wrote nearly twenty-five years ago, "One of the little probed mysteries of social history is society's hostility to its greatest benefactors, the producers of wealth."[10] Most likely, this mystery of which Gilder speaks lies buried deep within the human heart.

The Invisible War over Fairness

While class warfare in America today is non-existent, another kind of war is going on, one that has had, and continues to have, potential implications for our perceptions of economic fairness. This war has been fought on many different battlefields and at many different levels of intensity over the past few decades. From our cable news television stations to our family dining room tables, this war goes on—and many of us aren't even aware of it. Sometimes it is right under our noses and we see it as something else. It also provides the fuel for the present class bias in our society.

This "invisible" war cuts across all classes and income groups, all race and ethnic groups, and involves many people who do not even realize they are participants in it. Because of this, the affects of this war are considerably more insidious than class warfare—and the social stakes are much higher. This war's reward is the future direction of society —insofar as what we believe about economic fairness.

The war has had many names over the years, and its battles have had many names. Its most popular name, of course, has been the culture war, and its battles carry the names of the particular armies involved. These are all too familiar if one only stops and looks back in time at the social protest movements that mushroomed since the 1960s. Beginning with the civil rights movement and leading on to the student and youth movements associated with the Vietnam War, they were followed by movements demanding feminist rights, environmental rights, gay and lesbian rights, and so on. In subsequent decades, new armies of social protesters emerged. These armies proclaimed abortion rights, rights for welfare mothers and single parents, rights for animals, and even children's rights. In most recent years, anti-globalists and anarchists have enlisted in the struggle.

The idea of a culture war in America, of course, is not new.[11] What is new, however, is this. We have all witnessed the various battles (i.e., the demonstrations, protests, picketing) in this war, but we have failed to realize that an "invisible" war about economic fairness has been taking place as well—behind the scenes so to speak. In my opinion, some of the movements that focus on various social issues have a vague, but common sentiment running through them: Anti-capitalism! The injustices being protested are rooted, ultimately, in our economic system, capitalism.

Immediately, one might take issue with this and suggest that they know many capitalists and free marketers who endorse certain movements, both social and political, that our critical of our economic system. That is no doubt true. But it is in this lending of their active support to "movements" where we can find the common sentiment. Many of these movements of the late twentieth century are protesting injustices of one sort or another—and their common bond is victimization. And as mentioned earlier, where there is a victim there is also a culprit. Who is to blame? In most cases, the culprit is identified as someone with control or power—someone with money and wealth. Consequently, it is an easy step to turn quickly and point the finger of accusation at those who have economic power.

The affect of this myopia among the many adherents of today's various protest movements is to provide the rest of society with an easy guide for deciding what is and is not economically fair and just. Turn on the television and watch the latest protest to find out who is the culprit: big oil, pharmaceutical companies, CEOs, the greedy rich, and on and on. It is not that *all* protests and social movements have missed their mark; indeed, many have produced a much better society. For example, how can one argue over the moral rightness of the civil rights movement and aspects of the environmentalist or feminist movements. The problem is that, given man's basic sensitivities, self-choice is frequently blinded by social-choice—and the perception of economic fairness becomes blurred.

The impact of a culture war on the perception of economic fairness, therefore, represents only a manifestation of a greater struggle going on in all Americans (as well as other citizens of the modern world). It is a deeper and penetrating struggle within each and every one of us involving our individual sovereignty. Has "self" become subservient to "society," or "society" become subservient to "self?"

The 1960s and Social Revolution

The decade of the 1960s is perhaps the best-remembered of the last half-century—and its history has been told and retold. In essence, what happened, quite simply, was a social revolution—a revolution whose effects we feel to this very day.

The ingredients of the social revolution of the 1960s were demographic, economic, and social in nature. Their confluence in that decade may have gone largely unnoticed had it not been for two events that served as the catalysts of the revolution—the civil rights movement and the Vietnam War.

The demographic ingredient, of course, was the maturing of the baby boom generation in the 1960s. Of the 75 million or so babies born between 1946 and 1964, a significant proportion of them were in their teenage years and early twenties during the 1960s.[12] The economic ingredient was the economic prosperity enjoyed by Americans in these years. The

Federal income tax cut of President Kennedy provided the nation with a springboard to strong economic growth during the decade.[13] And finally, the social ingredient was the awakening (which really began in the 1950s) of a social conscience on the part of many young persons—a conscience that eschewed conformity and traditional values because of the materialism, bigotry, and hypocrisy that they believed were embedded in American life.[14] These three ingredients, when mixed together, produced a youthful, affluent, and restless segment of society, which, when confronted with the growing military conflict in Vietnam and growing civil rights demonstrations, erupted into anti-social behavior.

Other social concerns piqued this youthful segment of society. Nuclear bomb testing, the military-industrial complex, urban and rural poverty, the wasting of the earth's resources, the profit motive, and other societal insensitivities were swirling about the consciences of much of American youth at that time. Tom Hayden, in his 1962 Port Huron manifesto of the Students for a Democratic Society (SDS), pointed to many of these "paradoxes" (as he called them), which confronted young people and students.[15]

The seeds of anti-capitalism were also quite evident in Hayden's SDS statement. References to the inequalities of wealth and income, the "sapping" of earth's physical resources, the need to work for other purposes than simply money and profit, and the necessity to allocate resources on the basis of need, all reveal an anti-capitalist sentiment. Indeed, the manifesto suggests that to solve these many disturbing paradoxes a greater involvement of the public sector (i.e., government) was required as well as a vigorous advocacy on the part of the new left.

The rest of the story of the 1960s (and early 1970s) is well-known. Protest groups of all kinds grew in number, their core interests being the anti-war and civil rights movements. But as the Vietnam War wound down and the civil rights movement became less energized, other groups spun off and splintered, some quite specifically anti-capitalist, such as the Symbionese Liberation Army, and others less so. Nevertheless, a basic commonality of all of them could be found in their purpose, if one looked hard enough: anti-capitalism.

The Philosophic Basis of the Social Revolution

Human history is a nothing more than a long thread. Consequently, it can be said that what happened in the 1960s was nothing more than the further evolution of a well-known political philosophy: liberalism. Liberalism, at its core, is the belief that man is a free being, that is, man is autonomous and rational, free from any authority and tradition.

But how free is free?

As various political philosophers over the centuries expanded on this core belief, it became evident that liberalism was an evolving philosophy. An important development in liberalism's evolution was the distinction made between negative and positive liberty in the context of government's role in society.[16] Basically, negative liberty means that an individual is free to the extent that no one or nobody interferes with his activities. Positive liberty, on the other hand, means an individual is free when he has acted according to his true will, or self-actualization. In both instances, the "self" is central, and the role of government may be viewed as a hindrance in the first instance and a help in the second. In the former case, the important point for the individual is the protection of one's right to act, while in the latter, the important point is the actualization of one's own true nature.

For many years prior to the decade of the 1960s, negative liberty was slowly losing its influence in the evolution of modern liberalism while positive liberty was slowly becoming more influential. The "shifting of the rudder" of this political philosophy would profoundly affect how the question, "How free is free?" was answered. Indeed, the answer became most obvious in the 1960s and as subsequent decades unfolded, especially for the young. The answer was quite simply: Do what you want to do!

Robert Bork, the conservative scholar, wrote about the liberalism of the 1960s—and its lack of limits:

> Our modern, virtually unqualified, enthusiasm for liberty forgets that liberty can only be "the space between the walls," the walls of morality and the law based upon morality. It is sensible to argue how far apart the walls should be set, but it is cultural suicide to demand all space and no walls.[17]

A Surrendering of "Self"

As is often mentioned in political commentary, the liberalism of the late twentieth century (and today) was much different than the liberalism of the nineteenth century. In simplest terms, while the "self" remained at the core of liberalism, the *modus operandi* for making liberty manifest in one's life changed. The individual was supplanted by the group. As the nation matured, it became more expedient for achieving individual interests by working collectively. Many voices shouting at the government were better than just one voice. The women's suffrage movement and the trade and industrial union movement were early examples and the shift became particularly pronounced in the second half of the twentieth century. The significance of this shift from individual action to collective action embodied within it, whether knowingly or unknowingly, a sentiment of anti-capitalism.

When one examines the social history of the closing decades of the twentieth century it becomes obvious that our society was "Balkanizing." Groups were multiplying rapidly—and their commonality was their victimization. Whatever banner a group was organizing under, individuals were coming together to complain about the grievances they had, caused by someone or something. It was the age of multiculturalism and the objective was clear: diversity was to be celebrated and injustices were to be corrected.

Man is a social animal, of course, and has always come together in groups of one kind or another, be it a tribe or a political party. Some thing or purpose binds them together—and in the 1960s it was an injustice or grievance. A number of these groups served a social and moral purpose, as mentioned above. Their problem, however, was that their goal demanded a subjugation of an individual's will. For correcting a grievance, therefore, a philosophic price had to be paid, and the subjugation of will, either knowingly or unknowingly, extended into other domains of the individual's self. Self-thought became collective-thought.

Capitalism, of course, is built on the individual and the individual's right to life, liberty, and happiness. A central tenet of this economic philosophy is "entrepreneurship," or the ability for someone to organize and operate an enterprise. By definition, such an activity is "self-oriented." Whether or not the stated goals or objectives of the groups of the 1960s and later decades were to bring down capitalism, a sentiment of anti-capitalism was, nevertheless, inherent in them. The spirit of entrepreneurship, which comes only from the individual, or self, is not found in the charters, constitutions, or mission statements of most of these groups and organizations. What is found, however, is a spirit of collective will to change society.

The surrendering of "self" to a group has (and had) a cathartic benefit that must not be overlooked. It is pleasurable because fault or guilt is externalized. For many members of such groups, personal failings or feelings of inadequacy could be easily deposited at the doorstep of the "someone or something" that was responsible for the grievances being protested.

The Counterrevolution

All social revolutions lead to counterrevolutions, just like the famous law of physics involving actions and reactions. The engine of the counterrevolution to the social revolution of the 1960s was quite simply, "time." As the decades changed, the baby boom generation matured, the economy grew, and society changed. While these developments were not as startling and newsworthy as the developments during the 1960s and early 1970s, the exhortations of the protest groups and organizations from that era slowly diminished.

Consider the babies born between 1946 and 1956, or the kids in the first half of the baby boom generation. By 1971, they ranged in age from approximately fifteen to twenty-four and had approached and (for some) reached adulthood during the tumultuous 1960s—the period of civil rights demonstrations, riots, the war in Vietnam, assassinations, and, in general, the "trashing of traditional values." No doubt, millions of these young people had been swept up in many of the events of that era and became, what was called back then, the "flower children" and the "hippies." By 2001, or thirty years later, this cohort of young people was forty-five to fifty-four years old and into middle age. According to the Census Bureau, in 2001 the median annual income (in 2001 dollars) of families in which the householder was age forty-five to fifty-four was $68,114 compared to a median of $52,275 for all families.[18] Obviously, this age group represents the part of the life cycle in which incomes reach their peak; nevertheless, this economic achievement for an age cohort which engendered considerable worry (and scorn) in the 1960s and early 1970s suggests that many of them eventually returned to the fold of traditional American values, or at least the economic ones.

Another unheralded part of the counterrevolution was the unrelenting growth of the nation's economy. Recessions and economic slowdowns did occur, of course, in the remaining decades of the twentieth century, but no one can dispute the fact that after thirty or forty years, the economic lives of all Americans were much better off in recent years than they were back then. Incomes were higher, wages were higher, job opportunities abounded, productivity growth had returned to levels not seen in decades, and we lived in better housing with electronic and telecommunication devices galore. Clearly, for those who spoke for changing a society "hung up" on materialism and consumerism, their message fell upon deaf ears. For those who decried the abject poverty of a large group of American citizens, the Census Bureau's poverty statistics indicated that the poverty rate was almost the same as it was thirty years earlier.[19] For those back then preaching the message of anti-capitalism, the evidence of their failed message could be found everywhere one looked.

The last element of the counterrevolution was the many social changes that have taken place in the last thirty years—some even in response to social protests. No one can really argue that *nothing* has changed with respect to civil rights for Blacks and Hispanics or the rights of women or the rights of gays and lesbians. Social strictures have been loosened. Furthermore, there is evidence that some of the negative social trends that skyrocketed in the 1960s, 1970s, and 1980s, like crime, divorce, and illegitimate births, appeared to level off or decline in the 1990s. No doubt the collapse of communism in the Soviet Union in the late 1980s and early 1990s gave pause to many of the protesters of a couple decades earlier.

Consequently, there is abundant evidence of an effective counterrevolution to the social revolution of the 1960s—even though some segments of society have not realized it and others would not acknowledge it. But no one can dispute the fact that the message or messages being shouted out decades ago can still be heard in some quarters. Once the genie gets out of the bottle, it's very difficult to get it back in.

The Culture and the Income Gap

Our society is a mixture of different groups of people with different beliefs but similar abilities to perceive economic fairness. Over the past several decades, the belief systems of these groups have been exposed to questions and challenges. Many of these questions and challenges have been directed at their concept of economic fairness in society, specifically, their feelings about self-interest and competition. Indeed, the idea has been put forth that our free market, capitalistic system has been injurious to many people in the nation, as well as the world.

Much of this anti-capitalist rhetoric of today was bred during the 1960s during the anti-war movement of that period. It was subtly nurtured in the following decades by a variety of social protest groups, sometimes as a subliminal part of the protest messages being proclaimed. Instances of it appeared in the far left wing of the political spectrum. For example, the "living wage" movement, which is an effort to enhance the Federal minimum wage with a higher pay rate, contains a subtle message that, while perhaps not anti-capitalistic, cannot be construed as pro-business.[20]

Expressions of anti-capitalism, both the subtle and not so subtle, have surged in recent years in reaction to two different events. The first involved the World Trade Organization (WTO) and their periodic meetings in various cities of the world concerning globalization. The second, of course, was the anti-war movement associated with the war in Iraq beginning in March of 2003. In both cases, disparate protests groups came together to express their outrage over the U.S. (and other countries) involvement in globalization and the war in Iraq. Groups as disparate as animal rights advocates and anarchist-syndicalist groups flooded the streets to express their dissent. Again, it is important to state that for some groups, anti-capitalism was not a part of their protest, even though their association with other groups espousing anti-capitalism would make it appear so—and this is the danger.

Protesting in our society has become a part of the culture. It has now gone beyond the point of simply being a political right protected by our Constitution, but rather has become an *opportunity* to attack our economic way of life. In other words, some members of society continue to answer the question, "How free is free?" by saying "It's as a free as you want it to be!" Indeed, the sentiment of anti-capitalism that has been unleashed over the years and infects some individuals in society now does not even require a group for its message to be heard.

The problem with the explicit anti-capitalist message preached by the social protest groups of the early twenty-first century is that, while these groups represent only a tiny fraction of society, their message "seeps" into the rest of society and reinforces class bias directed at the rich. Given the nature of the modern mainstream media (e.g., Internet, television, telecommunication), their message is transmitted around the world in seconds. Consider the demonstrations against the WTO meetings in Seattle and Genoa in the early part of this decade and the demonstrations that took place around the world in response to the U.S. involvement in Iraq. The news of these demonstrations was flashed to every corner of the world. Even though many of the groups were not explicitly proclaiming an anti-capitalist message, the implicit message was there, woven into a broader fabric of protest.

The slogans of these groups proclaimed so boldly, so nobly, so self-righteously: "No blood for oil!" and "War is not the answer!" And words like "property," "profit," and "market share" were expressions of the evildoers and reflected the selfishness of mankind. The penguins, the poplars, and the polar bears were raised almost to levels of idolatry. Disheveled protesters kneeled in prayer in the streets in front of cold, granite-faced office buildings along with their brethren at the teach-ins, sit-ins, die-ins, old-fashioned pickets, and boycotts obstructing the flow of life, because life was not fair according to them—and it was obvious who they were blaming.

These messages come flowing into our range of perception and the urge is either to do something or do nothing. Do they have a point? Is our economic system evil, creating all these inequalities in our lives, widening the income gap?

Ironically, the collectivists' screams of protest are directed at individuals, or the "self." The collectivists have come together to convince the self, besiege the self, that the self has been duped by an evil economic system and that the self can be made better if it only joins in their chorus of protest. This is the goal.

Many of us, of course, have seen the protests in years past; indeed, we were probably part of them. But then we grew up and settled down to living our lives in the post-Vietnam era—our ear always waiting for a Joni Mitchell or Peter, Paul and Mary protest song from the past. Another part of society, a much younger part, was not even around when the modern day protest movement was born. They have only heard about those days and marvel about how noble it was to "Stop the war!" and "Give peace a chance!" This is all very emotional stuff for many of them—and they are swept up into the next protest march or demonstration.

It is important for those observers of the social landscape not to be blinded by those at the edges of the picture, or the margins. The elite media love the margins because news is created there. If one looks directly at the whole landscape, however, one can see what happened. The "self" won! Self won because, basically, people are *selfish*, and not in the pejorative sense of the word. An old German proverb says it all: Life consists of wanting something! As materialistic as this sounds, the fact is, it is true. Human history is the proof. What happened in the closing decades of the last century was that the vast majority of Americans were introduced to unparalleled economic prosperity culminating in the late 1990s. Whether it was because of success on the job, greater productivity on the part of oneself, an additional wage earner in the family, or whatever, American families and households saw their economic well-being blossom. And they liked that, as selfish as that sounds. They realized, despite the preaching, protests, and pleas from the margins of society, that there was nothing wrong with becoming rich and becoming richer. It was not greed, because needs were expanding. Whose business was it if one felt the need for an SUV or a 4,500 square foot house or a cruise around the world? Was it wrong for our grandparents to need a telephone or an indoor toilet or a college education for their son? In the final analysis, self matters—it is inalienable, despite the efforts of the collectivists at the margins of society.

The invisible war, therefore, is being fought by a subculture of anti-capitalists against the "self." Although it has not been very successful in recent years, the antiglobalization movement as well as the recent anti-war movement over U.S. involvement in Iraq has given this subculture a renewed vigor. Even though a "disconnect" now exists in the inequality-fairness relationship (about which more will be said), the subculture continues to spread its message in the attempt to distort the resolute self's perception of economic fairness.

Summing Up

America has always been regarded as the land of opportunity and fair play around the world, despite the recent worldwide reaction to the war in Iraq. For this reason, Americans are regarded as "fair minded" people, even when it comes to economic matters. Obviously, there have been the instances of stealing, cheating, and corruption that have cut across the strata of society, but these instances have been the exception and not the rule.

Americans, because of our social, economic, and demographic heterogeneity, tend to make their judgments about economic fairness from different platforms, or predispositions. For example, some of the rich assess matters from a platform of "threat," while many from the lower class and poor do so from a platform of "suspicion," and for the broad middle class, several platforms may be involved, such as, "hope," "fear," and "status." From these platforms, Americans have applied, when necessary, the principle of "adjusted symmetry" to issues of economic *unfairness*—and then they go on strike, demand tax concessions, riot in the streets, or do whatever is required to adjust the scales of fairness as they perceive them.

A society as heterogeneous as America's has not been immune from class consciousness. Fortunately, this consciousness (and sometimes tension) has come and gone, simply reflecting the dynamics of a healthy and democratic country. In the closing decades of the last century, however, a "class bias" toward the rich has emerged. This bias has been fostered in part by the mainstream media because of the reported widening of the income gap and the social transgressions of the rich, such as their conspicuous consumption (e.g., trophy homes) and ethical transgressions (e.g., corporate malfeasance).

An example of promoting such a bias was seen in *The New York Times* a few years ago. It published an ad sponsored by the New York State Public Employees Federation—a labor union—saying that the rich in New York are "...helping themselves to big, fat tax cuts and tax loopholes..." while facilities for the mentally ill are being closed and the public should call their lawmakers to "Say no!" to this practice.[21] Such a sweeping indictment of the rich in New York promotes class bias, and distorts many Americans' perception of matters of economic fairness involving the rich.

The class bias of which is spoken here has, unfortunately, helped fuel the invisible war over economic fairness in this country. This war, of course, is part of a greater culture war being fought between certain groups and the rest of society. And one of the goals of these groups in the war is changing the economic system in this nation because of the inequalities and injustices it presumably produces. The banner they bring into this invisible war is inscribed, "Anti-capitalism!"

They have had their "ups and downs" in this war. Beginning as a social revolution in the 1960s, this subculture grew weary as time went on as many of its members aged and came back up into America's mainstream. The economic fruits of capitalism became too tempting. But then, as time passed, new groups and individuals dropped into the subculture, keeping the basic message—and goals—alive. This, sadly, is where we are today.

Dissent and protest have been a common characteristic of the United States throughout its history. Indeed, it has helped shape the many platforms, alluded to earlier, from which judgments are made concerning economic fairness in everyday life. It is a natural by-product of a free and democratic society—and it has helped to build this nation state. But we must be ever mindful of its power: For it is one thing to dissent and protest in hope of reforming our economic system, but quite another when the dissent and protest is about ripping it down.

Notes

1. For an entertaining treatment of these behaviors, see Robert L. Heilbroner, *The Worldly Philosophers,* 5th Ed., (New York: Simon and Schuster, 1980), pp. 40-60.
2. Adam Smith, *An Inquiry Into the Nature and Cause of the Wealth of Nations*, The Modern Library Edition (New York: Random House, Inc., 1937), p. 14.
3. Indeed, *The New York Times* believes class matters very much in current day America. It devoted a series of articles on the subject in 2005 and then converted them into a book. See *Class Matters*, by correspondents of *The New York Times* (introduction by Bill Kellor), (New York: Times Books Henry Holt, 2005).
4. A useful discussion on the origination of classes is found under the entry "class" in *The New Palgrave: A Dictionary of Economics*, John Eatwell, Murray Milgate, and Peter Newman (Eds.), (London: The MacMillan Press Limited, 1987) pp. 432-434.

5. This class structure was defined by the sociologist, Daniel W. Possides, and discussed by Joel M. Charon, *Sociology: A Conceptual Approach* (Boston: Allyn and Bacon, 1986), pp. 322-325.

6. John H. Hallowell and Jene M. Porter, *Political Philosophy: The Search for Humanity and Order* (Scarborough, Ontario: Prentice Hall Canada, Inc., 1997), p. 598.

7. Work stoppages, or strikes, hit a decade high in 1937 of 4,740. See U.S. Bureau of the Census, *Historical Statistics of the United States: Colonial Times to 1970*, Series D 970, p. 179.

8. Not so many years ago, of course, segments of the middle class and the rich manifested biases toward the "undeserving" poor—and perhaps still do.

9. It should be mentioned that other parts of the lower and middle class, however, admire the rich. Simply consider the plethora of books, articles, and television shows devoted to the attributes of the rich as well as the "how to" books of becoming rich. Such media attention recognizes the fact that these "admirers" are convinced that upward economic mobility is a reality in America.

10. George Gilder, *Wealth and Poverty* (New York: Basic Books, Inc., Publishers, 1981), p. 96.

11. One of the many social observers who have addressed this issue from the political right, for example, is Patrick Buchanan. See Patrick J. Buchanan, *The Death of the West* (New York: St. Martin's Press, 2002).

12. A total of 75.9 million live births occurred between 1946 and 1964 compared to only 49.6 million in the earlier 18-year period. See U.S. Bureau of the Census, *Historical Statistics of the United States,* Series B 1, p. 49.

13. Gross national product increased by 4.0 percent a year or more in each year during the 1962-66 period. See U.S. Bureau of the Census, *Historical Statistics of the United States*, Series F 31, pp. 226-227.

14. See Sidney Lens, *Vietnam: A War on Two Fronts* (New York: Lodestar Books, 1990), p. 44.

15. The easiest way to read a copy of the Port Huron statement of 1962 is to access a Web page on the Internet that responds to the search command, "Students for a Democratic Society."

16. Isaiah Berlin wrote significantly on this topic in the second half of the twentieth century. See Isaiah Berlin, "Two Concepts of Liberty" in Isaiah Berlin, *Four Essays on Liberty* (London: Oxford University Press, 1969).

17. Robert H. Bork, *Slouching Towards Gomorrah* (New York: Regan Books, 1996), p. 65.

18. U.S. Census Bureau homepage, http://www.census.gov.

19. *Income, Poverty, and Health Insurance Coverage in the United States: 2006*, P60-233, U.S. Census Bureau, HHES Division (Washington, DC: USGPO, 2006), Table B-1, p. 44.

20. The Association of Community Organizations for Reform Now (ACORN) has a web page that promotes the "living wage" movement. See http://www.living-wagecampaign.org.

21. *The New York Times,* April 2, 2003, p. A29.

4

The Income Inequality–Economic Fairness "Disconnect"

> *I think that egalitarian ethical views are so deeply imbedded in culture that we often find it embarrassing to discuss the issue, and even to question the validity of that position.*
> —William H. Poole

The reason there is *not* a revolution in this country today over the income gap but only an income gap muddle is because of, the income inequality–economic fairness "disconnect" that took place over the last few decades.

Changes in income inequality and economic fairness have been traditionally thought to be inversely related. That is, as a society's income gap grows wider, the general level of economic fairness declines. In the parlance of the street, this translates to, "the rich are getting richer and the poor are getting poorer!"

It should be clear by now that the hypothesis underlying the message of this book is that the traditional relationship between inequality and fairness broke down in the United States. A "disconnect" developed. For many Americans, this disconnect has not been fully understood nor explained to them in a clear and concise way.

Much of our mainstream media, although never explicitly saying so, believe that the relationship between growing income inequality and declining economic fairness is still very much alive. Simply pick up a copy of the morning newspaper or watch the evening news and read the stories relating to the economic conditions of segments of our society and there, between the lines (and sometimes not between the lines), you will find the traditional relationship. Whether it is a story relating to the under-funded pension plans of retirees or the low-wage workers without health benefits, this relationship is lurking in the shadows. And as discussed earlier, it always conjures up victims and culprits.

This is because the media continues to subscribe wholeheartedly to the "growing inequality–declining fairness" relationship; and for many people, especially those in a muddle over the income gap, the "disconnect" has not been fully explained or understood. To read or listen to the commentary on growing income inequality provided by this nation's elite media in recent years would have one believe that economic hopelessness had spread across the land and economic envy was dripping from the mouths of millions of Americans.

What's an Income Gap *without* Envy?

We all have a fairly good idea of what envy is, and some of us, the more religious ones, probably have a better idea than others. To refresh the memories of those who have only a general recollection of it, the dictionary definition is this: Envy is a feeling of discontent and ill will because of another's advantages, possessions, etc.; resentful dislike of another who has something that one desires.[1]

Theologically, envy is a serious matter. Related to this, of course, are other disordered desires such as greed (i.e., amassing earthly goods without limit) and avarice (i.e., a passion for riches and their attendant power). In our popular media we have seen these latter terms used quite regularly by social critics to characterize those people at the upper end of our income distribution. But it is to envy one must look, and especially among the poor and middle class, if we wish to find evidence of the consequences of this country's widening income gap. Shouldn't envy be rampant if our income gap is immorally wide?

The problem is how do you measure envy? Again, it is like one of those human behaviors that cannot really be quantified. How do you measure love or hate, fear or anger, for example? The best that can be done is to observe the expressions of these emotions, or their *manifestations*, in this case the manifestations of envy.

There hasn't been much evidence in the past of the poor and middle class lashing out at the rich, and manifesting their envy in that way. Without doubt, envy of the rich and the well-to-do exists in the hearts of many people, but in today's world it is more likely to be expressed through expressions of class bias, or in its subtler form, class consciousness.

The argument is not that today's level of income inequality is at its ideal or optimal size. One economist has suggested that an ideal income distribution is one that is "envy free," in other words, one in which each income class prefers its own share of the income pie to the others' shares.[2] Another believed that an ideal income distribution was one in which each income class considered its share of the income pie to be just "enough," whatever the amounts.[3] No, we are far from these ideals.

The point is that although we are far from attaining an ideal income distribution, the one we do have, including the income gap, is really not all that bad either (despite the persistence of poverty in our midst). And there is some indirect evidence of this fact in the public domain, and from of all places, *The New York Times.*

The *Times* conducted a survey during 2004 and 2005 and published a series of articles about class in America. Although the central point of their first article was that "...class is still a powerful force in American life" and economic mobility is far less than it once was thought, the survey results accompanying the story were not necessarily reflective of an envious society.[4] They *do not* reflect a society filled with envy as the result of outsourced jobs, miserly paychecks, a future without health insurance and retirement benefits, and a widening income gap. Here are some of the highlights:

- 80 percent of the respondents believed it was still possible to start out poor, work hard, and become rich compared to only about 60 percent 30 years ago;
- 45 percent believed their current class to be higher than it was when they were growing up;
- and 40 percent said the likelihood of moving up from one social class to another was greater today than it was 30 years ago.[5]

It would appear that the *Times* article was attempting "to put some tears on a smiley face" by saying that despite these optimistic responses on the part of Americans, *experts* suggest that upward economic mobility has declined in America over the years. These experts, most of whom are economists, contend that it is more difficult for Americans to move up the economic ladder because of the widening income gap, which has "deepened the hidden divisions of class."

Economic mobility, as even the *Times* article mentions, is a difficult concept to measure, especially when it comes to whether or not there is more or less mobility today than in years gone by. But regardless of that issue, the survey results are not indicative of a society about to rip itself apart because of the envy produced from growing income differences. Indeed, the survey results from members of our society were upbeat and hopeful about their economic future.

In response to a question concerning whether survey respondents will reach the American dream in their lifetimes, a majority said that they already had reached it or would some day—and this was true whether household income was under $30,000 a year or over $100,000. The absence of an increase in the level of "envy" at a time of growing income differences is *inconsistent* with the traditional inverse relationship between inequality and fairness. So what's going on?

It's a "Disconnect"

Of course there are degrees of envy. There are millions of envious people in the nation who would love to have that penthouse on Fifth Avenue or that yacht out there on the bay or that Rolls Royce coming down the street. But this type of envy is what could be called "good" envy. These people really don't resent the people who own that penthouse or yacht or Rolls Royce. Indeed, this type of envy could instill in individuals a desire to go out and strive for those material possessions. In contrast, the "bad" envy not only produces a desire to have the luxuries of others but it also creates a strong resentment towards the owners of those luxuries.[6]

It is the bad envy that leads to social instability and turmoil. This bad envy can be easily created in people if their sense of fairness or fair play has been violated. If something is viewed as not being "fair" in the economic lives of people, bad envy is quite likely to follow. So, while it has been helpful to look at the survey results of the *Times* mentioned above regarding manifestations of envy, it is perhaps even more important to find some evidence about economic fairness in America—and contrast that with growing income inequality.

Recall, the traditional relationship between income inequality and economic fairness has always been thought to be inverse, that is, the more inequality the less fairness or the less inequality the more fairness. This has been and continues to be the interpretation of most of our mainstream media, whether newspapers, cable and network news, magazines, and even public broadcasting.

As was the case with envy, however, measuring society's feelings about economic fairness is problematic. Most economists deplore even discussing such amorphous phenomenon like "economic fairness," no less attempting to measure it. But not all. A good number of readers of this book have heard of the Consumer Confidence Index produced every month by the Conference Board in New York City. This statistic presumably quantifies how much confidence consumers have in the short-term economic future (i.e., jobs, interest rates, wages). And some readers have no doubt heard of the Misery Index, especially during Presidential election campaigns, which combines the unemployment rate and inflation rate into one statistic to reflect how much "so-called" economic misery Americans are experiencing. Consequently, approximations of such phenomenon, like economic fairness, are always feasible.

It is in this spirit that the following economic fairness index is presented. In simplest terms it is this:

$$\text{Economic Fairness Index} = 1.00 - \text{The Poverty Rate}$$

Or in other words, the economic fairness index is equal to the nation's "nonpoverty" rate—the proportion of the population *not* poor.

Clearly, the choice for a fairness index is arbitrary. It is believed by this author, however, that poverty in a society, and most importantly, its absence (nonpoverty) is a useful approximation of economic fairness in a modern, democratic society since it reflects the extent to which human suffering brought about by the society's economic system will be tolerated. Accordingly, the justification of this fairness index is no more or no less rigorous than those of the previously two mentioned indexes.

The U.S. Census Bureau has measured "income" poverty of American families for many years through the Current Population Survey (CPS).[7] In addition, researchers have made comparable estimates of poverty stretching back to the early twentieth century. By combining the data from these two sources it is a simple matter to construct an economic fairness index—1.00 minus the poverty rate—or, in other words, the proportion of the nation's population that is *not* in poverty.[8] The trend in this economic fairness index across the last century can be observed in Figure 4.1 (a measure of 1.0 would represent a perfect economically fair society while a measure of 0.0 would represent a perfect economically unfair society).

The measurement of income inequality—or the income gap—across the same time period is much less problematic in the sense that income differences are easier to measure than economic fairness. Again, the U.S. Census Bureau has collected annual income information on American families in their CPS since immediately after WWII. From the distribution of these annual incomes the Bureau calculated Gini indexes, one of the more common measures of income inequality that it produces. Academic researchers have also made estimates of the Gini index back to the early twentieth century so it is possible to combine the two series to cover the entire twentieth century.[9] The trend in income inequality over the last century is also presented in Figure 4.1 (a Gini index of 1.0 represents a perfectly unequal distribution of income in society while an index of 0.0 represents a perfectly equal distribution of income).

These measures of income inequality (the Gini index) and economic fairness (the nonpoverty rate), therefore, are "proxies" for assessing the inverse relationship between inequality and fairness. By examining the trends in the measures it will be possible to see the "disconnect" in the inequality-fairness relationship that occurred in the second half of the last century.

The trends in both indexes appear to be mirror images of one another in the 1900 to 1950 period. For example, income inequality, which was very high in the early years of the last century, tended to rise slowly as WWI approached and fairness appeared to slump. With the onset of war, however, both indexes reversed directions. During the 1920s, the income gap began widening rapidly and peaked in the early 1930s at the same time economic fairness was dropping like a rock. Through the rest of the 1930s and into the 1940s, inequality declined while the index of economic fairness improved dramatically. An inverse relationship between inequality and fairness was clearly evident during the first half of the century.

After the 1950s, the near mirror image between the two indexes becomes much less apparent. The downward trend in the inequality of incomes, as measured by the Gini index, tended to stabilize relative to earlier years and then began to edge upward over the last three decades of the century. In sharp contrast, the fairness index, as measured by the nonpoverty rate, continued its upward climb in the 1950 to 1970 period reaching nearly 0.9. It then stabilized for the rest of the century, but with minor decreases in years associated with recessions and increases in years of economic expansion. Evidence of an inverse relationship between changes in income inequality and economic fairness are much more difficult to discern in the second half of the century and especially in the years over the 1970 to 2000 period.

Another way to observe this "disconnect" in the inequality-fairness relationship is to statistically measure the strength (correlation) and nature (inverse vs. direct) of the relationship over the first and second halves of the century. Two scatter diagrams containing the data from Figure 4.1 are displayed in Figures 4.2a and 4.2b, along with the estimated regression lines.

From the two panels of the figure it becomes obvious that the relationship between inequality and fairness (as defined here) had changed between the first half and second half of the last century. In the first half

Figure 4.1
Gini and Fairness Indexes
1900 to 2000

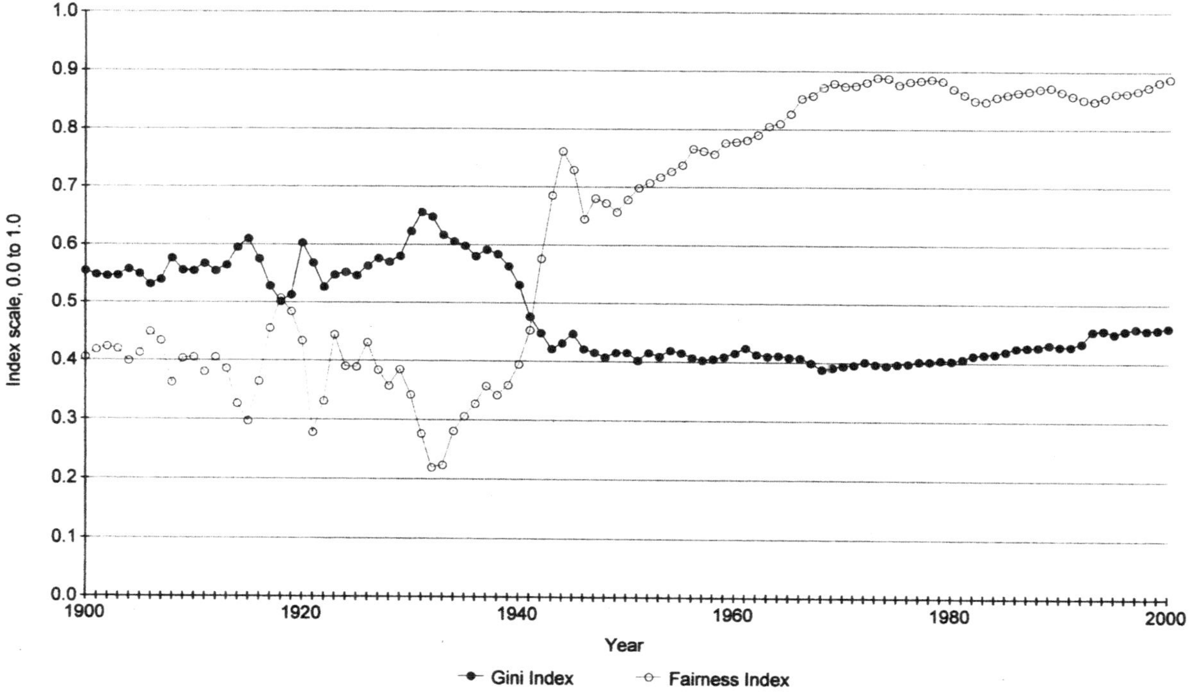

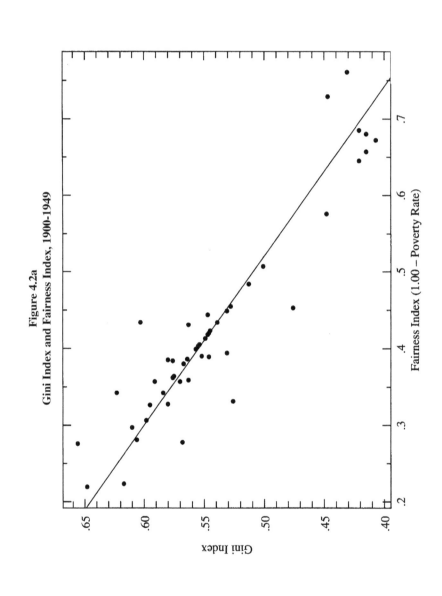

Figure 4.2a
Gini Index and Fairness Index, 1900-1949

Figure 4.2b
Gini Index and Fairness Index, 1950-2000

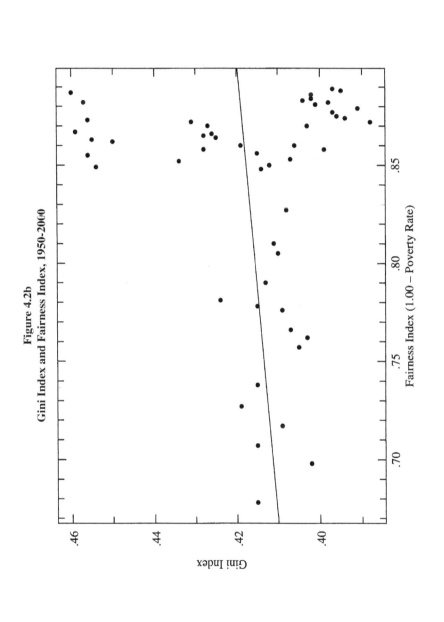

the relationship was clearly inverse, that is, when inequality rose, fairness declined and vice versa. This, of course, is the traditional view of the relationship—which is believed to exist today by much of the media as well as others on the political left. In addition, the relationship was a relatively strong one as indicated by how the "plot points" are closely clustered to the regression line (the coefficient of correlation was -.93).

In the second half of the century, on the other hand, the scatter diagram reveals that the relationship appeared to be a "mildly" direct one, that is, when inequality stabilized or rose slightly, economic fairness rose as well or did not change much. This represents the disconnect, or breakdown, in the traditional relationship. Furthermore, the relationship had now become relatively weak since the plot points are not clustered near the regression line (the coefficient of correlation was only .15). Indeed, the plot points tend to spread away from the regression line when the fairness index moved above .85, or a poverty rate of 15 percent.

These statistical findings about a disconnect in an age-old economic relationship are subject to dispute, of course, just as any controversial finding. Different measures of inequality and fairness could be used leading to different conclusions. But when the statistical and non-statistical dimensions surrounding the income gap are combined, the conclusion appears incontrovertible: the relationship between inequality and fairness, as defined here, had broken down.

It is difficult, of course, to cast off traditional ways of thinking about such things as inequality and fairness. But an unfortunate aspect of this statistical finding is that the mainstream media has failed to recognize it and inform its readers and listeners. Instead, it appears they have perpetuated this traditional relationship in contemporary America.

Our Evolving "Social Contract"

The concept of a "social contract" has been frequently in the news. In its popular usage, it implies some agreement between a society and its governing or "power" authority. In the context of the traditional growing income inequality–declining economic fairness relationship, a widening income gap would suggest that the social contract has been violated and is imperiled. The consequences, presumably, are growing social discontent and instability.

Philosophers, economists, sociologists, and many other observers of humankind have pondered the whys and wherefores of social disintegration and breakdown. Expressions of discontent, of course, can originate not only as a result of economic changes but also because of political changes, religious persecutions, or other events affecting a significant part of a society. Central to all of these expressions of discontent is some sense of growing repression. As one sociologist put it, "The immediate cause of revolution is always the growth of repression of the main instincts of the majority of society, and the impossibility of obtaining for those instincts the necessary minimum of satisfaction."[10]

It is difficult to know how far, today, subscribers to the traditional view of the inequality-fairness relationship believe we have come down the path toward social disorder. If they are perfectly honest, they would probably answer, "not very far." This is because they can very well observe the relative social equanimity that exists in contemporary American society, even despite growing fears of a recession.

From the reportage of the media, however, it is easy to conclude that the elite media are not very optimistic. Those subscribing to the traditional relationship, no doubt believe that this nation's social contract has been imperiled, or at least that part of it dealing with the economic aspects of the contract. In all fairness to them, they probably hope that the social contract could be amended, or renegotiated, therefore, preventing social erosion.

To understand their thinking, it is important to consider the concept of a society's "social contract." Social contracts, of course, are abstract conceptions but, nevertheless, suggest some agreement among individuals. That is, if we do this or forgo from doing that, than we can expect something in return from the other party we have the contract with. In one of its original formulations by the seventeenth-century English philosopher Thomas Hobbes, a social contract was conceived as a means of human self-preservation.[11] Hobbes viewed man's natural state as basically one of war with his fellow man. To rid oneself of this perpetual state—and survive—the only thing to do was to refrain from such violence *if* in return his neighbor would do likewise.

The notion of a social contract has gone through numerous re-conceptions over the centuries. John Locke, Jean-Jacques Rousseau, and other philosophers have expounded on the basic concept. It slowly took on the meaning of some sort of agreement between society and its governmental or power authority. In centuries past it may have taken the form of a king saying to his subjects, "if you work my fields and don't cause me any problems, I will protect you from the awful king in the next country beyond the mountains." In today's modern countries it is usually expressed as, "if you work hard, pay your taxes, and obey the laws, I (the government or power authority) will build you highways and schools, provide you with jobs and a nice retirement, and protect your borders."

Usage of the social contract concept (at least its economic aspects) has recently been applied in comparative analyses between the economies of Europe and the United States. Some European nations have social contracts (and currently undergoing reform) that have been referred to as "welfare" oriented in the sense that the government provides for the welfare of everyone "from cradle to crave" in exchange for highly regulated labor markets, high tax rates, and tight government control over many aspects of everyday life. In the United States, on the other hand, the social contract has a more "market" oriented meaning in which citizens are allowed to "fend for themselves" with the possibility of reaping large economic returns (e.g., high wages or salaries) or experiencing significant economic losses (e.g., losing a job and/or health insurance coverage) in return for lower tax rates and fewer rules and regulations.

The mainstream media and the other subscribers to the traditional view of the inequality-fairness relationship in our country, of course, believe the social contract has been breached. According to them, as income inequality has grown in society, segments of it have been left behind. Specifically, the poor, the working class, and the lower middle class (indeed, even everyone below the 90th income percentile) have not benefited to the same extent as the very rich—and they need help. The governing or power authority (and here the partners of the contract are assumed to include the corporations and employers as well) has played favorites and has not been fair to the less fortunate in society.

Calls for redefining our nation's social contract have been numerous and come from various sources. In general, they include requests for higher minimum wages, living wage provisions, universal health insurance coverage, and other social benefits for the lower half of the income distribution. Two very specific calls from respected academics and representatives of "think tanks" deserve attention.

The first was developed by Richard B. Freeman, a Harvard economist. He says it's time to get over what are the causes of the "new" income inequality and what are its effects—and begin dealing with the problem.[12] He suggests five amendments to the contract: let workers have control of their own pension funds, or in other words, re-distribute assets; shift social expenditures forward in the life-cycle (e.g., health insurance for all children); raise the "social" wage (i.e., a higher minimum acceptable income level); rebuild unions by making unionization easier to accomplish; and rebuild our cities (e.g., investing in the physical and social infrastructure). In summarizing his amendments Freeman says the unifying theme should be achieving equal opportunity through "leveling the playing field."

Rudolph Penner, Isabel Sawhill, and Timothy Taylor outlined another way of amending, or as they suggest, updating the social contract.[13] They viewed the focus of the updating to concern three issues: slow productivity growth; growing income inequality; and the retirement of the baby boom generation. All of these, of course, inevitably have an impact on the income distribution. But regarding inequality, specifically, they suggest more assistance for the working poor in the form of wage supplements, child care, and health care, all at the expense of the governing or power authority.

These prescriptions for amending America's social contract—as do all of them originating on the political left— have common threads running through them. First, of course, each begins with the premise that the inequality-fairness relationship was very much intact at the opening of the twenty-first century and that the social contract needs repair. Second, there is a commonality in the amendments to the contract that resembles in many ways the social contracts of Western European countries, for example, France and Germany. (Indeed, Richard Freeman's are explicitly modeled after certain European social assistance programs.) And third, the changes to the social contract that are prescribed all involve changes that must be made on the part of the governing or power authority and never on the part of the people. It is the former that must always reform, correct, and, most importantly, expand its role in the social contract.

So, the "way it's suppose to be" according to subscribers of the traditional inequality-fairness relationship might involve two possible paths. The first would be a renegotiation of this nation's social contract—beginning via the ballot box—moving closer to the economic model of the nations of the European Union. The second would be more drastic and possibly involve an agonizing period of social instability and discord until the governing-power authority is forced—via the ballot box and the will of the people—to simply restructure our economic system.

The first path involves billions and billions of dollars in social expenditures—and convincing the American electorate that this is the way to go. But the fiscal and economic difficulties confronting many Western European nations today is sufficient evidence of the difficult consequences that the first path might lead to. Indeed, in 2007, the newly elected President of France, Nicolas Sarkozy, campaigned on reforming many of his nation's generous social programs, moving *away* from his nation's liberal social contract. The second path, of course, is highly unlikely in the United States because social unrest, even in times of recent recessions, has been at very low levels.

But the effort to push on down the first path continues. It continues unabashedly under the auspices, primarily, of the mainstream and elite media of the nation. How else does one explain the appearance of *The New York Times* series of articles in 2005 (mentioned earlier) about the hardening of class divisions in America? Here is a nation, viewed as the economic leader of the world and the envy of many nations around the world, being told by one of its own premier newspapers that one's chances of economic success in America were slowly diminishing—this despite the survey results from Americans expressing economic optimism in the very same news story.

Social contracts, of course, are always being altered, modified, and adapted to social and economic realities. Indeed, one could say they evolve. This was, of course, quite evident in the first half of the last century when this nation grappled with two world wars and the Great Depression. The social contract of pre-WWI years was far different from the one in place in the post-WWII years. The contract was reworked and renegotiated with the consent of *both* the governing-power authority and the people. Both parties to the contract conceded and acceded to the demands of the others.

But it is critical to distinguish between events that you might think will or will not change the social contract. For example, the Congressional elections of 2006, when the Democratic Party took control of both the Senate and House of Representatives from the Republican Party, might have been construed as the beginning of such a change—and I'm sure many Democrats, liberals, and left-leaning citizens believed this to be the case. While social contracts do change, however, change is slow and ever so gradual. Political parties, for example, have their very obvious cyclical paths; political, philosophical, and cultural attitudes are more subtle and difficult to discern over short periods of time.

Although the 2006 election results indicated a call for "change," it is not yet evident by late 2007 and early 2008 that the present social contract is about to be "rewritten" in terms calling for more governmental intervention in our lives. The causes of the 2006 political shift are still being debated, especially because of the dominance of the war in Iraq as an issue. Irrespective of the 2006 election results and even the "predicted" Democratic landslide in 2008, there is still a belief that the body politic over the last few decades has shifted in a more conservative direction—and today's social contract reflects this. More is now asked of, and expected of, the "other" party to the contract—the people. *Personal* responsibility for one's own life has emerged and vies for attention with *social* responsibility for one's fellow man. Simply consider the passage of the welfare reform legislation of the mid-1990s and the significant decline of unionization in the work force, as examples. Millions of Americans over the last thirty to forty years have come to the realization that they themselves are responsible for their own destiny and not the governing or power authority. In other words, emphasis in recent decades has shifted from the "collective-us" to the "individual-I." Whether we are on the doorstep of a reversal in this national view awaits to be seen.

The Future of the Disconnect

The evolving social contract of this nation is very much related to the traditional income inequality–economic fairness relationship, and the "disconnect" that took place in that relationship over the last few decades. But what about the future of this disconnect? Could the traditional relationship be re-established—and as the income gap widens further, economic fairness begins melting away?

Economic change, of course, is ever present, but America, as it moves further into the third full century of existence, is at a crossroads. The pendulum in our collective economic clock has moved from its social responsibility–social justice side to its personal responsibility–personal justice side, although it has much more distance to go to be sure. If it keeps moving in this direction, the traditional relationship between inequality and fairness will fade into the past and the disconnect will be marked in economic history as a significant event in the history of man. If not, the irony of ironies will occur—our society will, indeed, turn into a nation of haves and have nots.

Why?

The middle class, as it has expanded over recent decades, now spans an enormous "dollar distance" in terms of its annual household incomes—from the $25,000-$30,000 range all the way to $150,000 and even beyond. This distance reflects a great heterogeneity between those families in the upper middle class and those in the lower middle class. As will be explained in greater detail in the following chapter, this middle class expansion has been brought on by changes that have taken place in our society's "socio-economic dynamic."

The socio-economic dynamic of a nation represents nothing more than the choices that people make (see Appendix B for a more conceptual discussion). These choices involve our social relations, our demography, and our economy, as well as those that are interrelated. Consider some of the ordinary choices made in one's life cycle: schools, friends, jobs, where we live, who we marry. All of these choices, ultimately, influence what our position will be in the income distribution ten years from now, or where we are today.

The choices, or the requirements for choosing, have remained pretty much the same down through the years, but the *influences* on these choices are subject to change. Consider, for example, how to earn a living. One-hundred years ago, if I was lucky enough to have a high school education perhaps I could get a job in a store or a bank or work in a factory or a coal mine. Chances for further education were small. Fifty years ago I may have been able to get similar jobs, especially with the help of a union, or maybe even go to college or enter the Armed Forces and then go to school with the assistance of the GI Bill. And five years ago, I probably would be going onto college or an institution of higher learning—if I truly wanted a future job from which I could support myself.

Consider other choices to be made. Whether or not to marry now or later, have children or not, divorce or separate? Whether to take a loan out to start a business or buy a house? Whether to change jobs now or stick it out with my present employer? All of them, to varying degrees, have important consequences for our economic success or failure. Again, the influences affecting our choices differ from one time period to another.

This is why the current day "socio-economic dynamic" differs from the one of the 1960s and 1970s, which in turn differs from the one of the 1940s and 1950s, which in turn differs from the one of the 1920s and 1930s, and on and on. Life cycle choices and decisions will always be made but under ever changing socio-economic dynamics. Indeed, the social, demographic, and economic choices made by humans can be thought of as tectonic plates lying beneath the earth's surface.[14] These sets of choices—the tectonic plates—are very slow to change but they do change. Furthermore, they interact with one another, colliding, slipping above or below one another, moving further apart, always however, reshaping the landscape above, or, if you will, the income distribution. In the process, income inequality rises and falls, and like the seismologists, the economists measure the "ups and downs" and attempt to understand why the economic landscape has changed as it has.

If the social contract of this nation is renegotiated along the lines suggested by the mainstream media and others who still believe in the traditional relationship between inequality and fairness, the influences affecting today's socio-economic dynamic (or tectonic plates), I predict, will shift in such a way so as to produce a bi-modal income distribution. For the non-statisticians, this is a distribution containing two "humps," or ranges of annual incomes occurring most frequently. A hypothetical bi-modal distribution is shown in Figure 4.3.

In effect, what this income distribution implies is a hollowing out of the middle class—or a *true* separation between the lower and upper segments of the middle class. The reason for this is quite simple: With the host of social and economic programs put in place to aid the poor, working class, and middle class by the new governing authority, economic incentive would slowly deteriorate. Upward economic mobility would come to a standstill because Adam Smith's invisible hand would now have become visible—but in the form of a "handout."

Hopefully, the social contract will not be renegotiated along the lines being suggested by the political left. Indeed, I hope it will continue to be reformulated but in the guise of individuals assuming more and more responsibility for their own economic welfare. In other words, because of the new socio-economic dynamic people will take a more active role in the social contract rather than the governing authority. What will hap-

Figure 4.3
A Bi-Modal Income Distribution

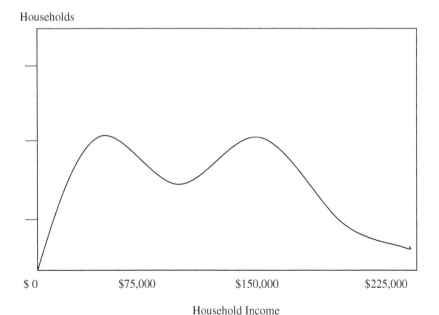

Households

$ 0 $75,000 $150,000 $225,000

Household Income

pen to the income distribution is that it will continue to shift further and further to the right with more and more households joining the ranks of the upper middle class. This will represent the continuation of the second middle class revolution in America.

Notes

1. *Webster's New World Dictionary of the American Language*, Second College Edition, (New York: Simon & Schuster, 1980), p. 468.
2. Hal Varian, "Equity, Envy, and Efficiency," *Journal of Economic Theory*, 9(1), pp. 63-91.
3. Harry Frankfurt, "Equality as a Moral Ideal," *Ethics*, October, 1987, pp. 21-43. Frankfurt refers to this as the "doctrine of sufficiency," and contrasts it to another ideal income distribution, one of equality.
4. "Class in America: Shadowy Lines That Still Divide," Janny Scott and David Leonhardt, *The New York Times*, May 15, 2005, pp. 1, 16, 17, and 18. The survey was based on telephone interviews conducted with 1,764 adults over the March 9-14, 2005 period, with an over-sampling of low income and high income households.
5. *Ibid.*, p. 16.
6. This distinction between a "good" and "bad" envy parallels a later discussion (in Chapter 8) about good and bad income inequality.
7. See Appendix A for a discussion of the CPS and the poverty measure.
8. Poverty data were obtained from *Poverty in the United States: 2001*, (P60-219), U. S. Bureau of the Census, HHES Division (Washington, DC: USGPO, September 2002), Appendix A, Table A-1, p. 21, and from Robert D. Plotnick, Eugene Smolensky, Erik Evenhouse, and Siabohan Reilly, "The Twentieth Century Record of Inequality and Poverty in the United States," in *The Cambridge Economic History of the United States, Vol. 3*, eds. Stanley L. Engerman and Robert E. Gallman (Cambridge, UK: Cambridge University Press, 2000), Appendix D, Table 4.4, pp. 292-294. Plotnick et al projected the poverty rate among persons back to 1914 using regression analyses and the author extended the projection back to 1900.
9. Gini indexes were obtained from *Money Income in the United States: 2001*, (P60-218), U.S. Bureau of the Census, HHES Division (Washington, DC: USGPO, September 2002), Appendix A, Table A-2, p. 19, and from Robert D. Plotnick et al (see footnote 8 above). As with the poverty rates, Plotnick et al projected the Gini index using regression analyses back to the early part of the twentieth century and the author extended the projection back to 1900.
10. Pitirim A. Sorokin, *The Sociology of Revolution* (New York: Howard Fertig, 1967 edition), p. 367.
11. John H. Hallowell and Jene M. Porter, *Political Philosophy: The Search for Humanity and Order* (Scarborough, Ontario: Prentice Hall Canada, Inc., 1997), p. 313.
12. Richard B. Freeman, *The New Inequality: Creating Solutions for Poor America* (Boston: Beacon Press, 1995), pp. 4-5.
13. Rudolph G. Penner, Isabell V. Sawhill, and Timothy Taylor, *Updating America's Social Contract* (New York: W.W. Norton & Company, 2000).
14. Lester Thurow, the well-known economist, employed a "tectonic plate" analogy in one of his many books to explain how the future of capitalism is being shaped. See Lester C. Thurow, *The Future of Capitalism* (New York: William Morrow, 1996), p. 8.

5

America's Evolving Middle Class

Upper classes are a nation's past; the middle class is its future.
—Ayn Rand

One of the most awe-inspiring stories of America over the last 100 years or so is the story of its middle class. If this nation can be referred to as the "melting pot," its middle class can be thought of as the "dish" that was being prepared in that pot for all these many years.[1]

America's middle class has been a well studied and a much discussed topic. The term conjures up many different images: Archie Bunker and his family, Norman Rockwell's paintings of a Thanksgiving dinner, Chevrolets and Fords, rows and rows of "cookie cutter" style houses in the suburbs, and parking lots full of cars at suburban shopping malls. But its depiction can be just as varied by the sociologists, economists, and others who have struggled with attempts to define it over the years. And the definition of the middle class is at the heart of much of the past debate over its economic health.

While striving for a satisfactory definition of America's middle class can be elusive at first, it is helpful and useful to sit back and simply reflect upon the process that was involved in the formation of what we commonly think of as this segment of our society. Since so many Americans consider themselves as middle class, this means thinking about us, for example, you and me.

The first thing that comes to mind probably is immigration. The wave of immigrants flocking to this nation's shore over the years has certainly been important even though we just didn't become middle class upon jumping off the boat. The second thing that pops into our heads is probably the jobs that our grandparents and parents worked at for so many years—struggling to make ends meet. Then, of course, there comes education. Pictures of the proud high school graduates come to mind or those of college students with their school names on the sweatshirts; or even the memories of learning, on the job, how to set bricks or plaster a wall. A fourth aspect in our retrospection may be the various apartments or houses our parents and their parents lived in: the overstuffed furniture in the living room; the first television set; indoor plumbing; and electric lights. Then, of course, there is the family: the marriage to the girl or boy next door; the babies; the divorces and separations; the death of the one who got the whole family started. One can go on, but the point is obvious: to get where we are, and especially if we call ourselves middle class, involved many processes—physical movements from place to place, job changing, studying, and so on. This point was briefly discussed in the previous chapter and it was called the "socio-economic dynamic."

As the reader has observed, a current-day definition of the middle class was put forward earlier—a purely monetary one. This definition was hinted at in the opening chapters. It was defined as any household whose annual income (in current dollars) fell between $25,000 and $150,000 (and perhaps higher)—a very wide range. But, of course, a realistic definition of the middle class would involve more dimensions than just annual income. For example, what about one's occupation, education, and wealth—three other common elements for defining socio-economic status. Then there are more subtle variables, such as family lineage, religious affiliation, cultural interests, and leisure time activities. All of these could be woven into a definitional matrix for determining whether an individual is from America's middle class.

The inevitable problem with any combination of these variables is that there is always an exception—someone or some family that just doesn't qualify for the middle class label even though they meet all the requirements. Pigeonholing humans on the basis of various attributes is always hazardous because of the complexity of the species. This is why the topic of the socio-economic dynamic has been raised. Because if attributes can only take us so far in identifying who is and who is not middle class, then perhaps the processes associated with *becoming* middle class can take us a little further.

It is for this reason that the word "morphing" will be used to describe the process of accessing this nation's middle class over the last thirty or forty years. The socio-economic dynamic operating in recent years has become so complicated relative to earlier eras of the nation's history that the result was an unusual expansion and transformation of our middle class. Morphology, of course, is the study of form and structure of an organism considered in its totality. By examining that part of our socio-economic dynamic applicable to the middle class, it is possible to understand how, by the beginning of the twenty-first century, the vast majority of families and households in this country identified themselves to be from the middle class.

The Socio-Economic Dynamic and Becoming Middle Class

Over the last century or so, there have been five identifiable socio-economic dynamics, which operated in American society.[2] They cover roughly the following time periods: 1870 to 1900; 1900 to 1930; 1930 to 1955; 1955 to 1975; 1975 to 2000.

The distinguishing feature of the first period—toward the end of the nineteenth century—was the dominance of the railroad in American life and the closing of the frontier; between 1900 and 1930, the distinguishing feature was the industrialization and urbanization of the nation; from 1930 to 1955, the key feature, without doubt, was the economic chaos and social disruption brought on by the Great Depression and World War II; during the twenty years between 1955 and 1975 the overriding feature was social "soul searching" and "reassessment"; and from 1975 to the end of the last century, the dominant features were the computer, globalization, and, quite simply, the economic quest for "more."

Whatever the period and whatever the key feature of the period, the same broad social, economic, and demographic factors of the socio-economic dynamic—*but each with varying degrees of influence during the period*—were shaping the society we lived in and our income distribution. And, within each of these periods, the American middle class was defining itself and redefining itself through these very same factors—*but each with varying degrees of influence during the period.* Before examining these periods in greater detail, the various social, economic, and demographic factors that have influenced the choices that determined our position in the income distribution are presented in Table 5.1.

All of these factors can be thought of in a "static" sense, that is, one is either a citizen or not, married or single, holds a job or does not. So, too, are the various interactions, that is, one is either an immigrant who is single and without a job, or some other combination. (Obviously, there are additional sub-factors below each major factor, for example, under job could be the category of a union or nonunion job.) All of these factors are associated with one's position in the income distribution and help to identify the *process* through which one reached that position—and of primary interest—reached the middle class.

Table 5.1
Social, Economic, and Demographic Factors
Associated with the Socio-Economic Dynamic

Social	Economic	Demographic
Immigration/Nonimmig.	Job/Work	Family Size
Education	Occupation	Age/Sex
Culture	Industry	Urban/Rural
Religion	Wealth	Race/Ethnic Origin
Government	Income Sources	Marital Status

As we examine each of the specific periods above, and the process by which American middle class status was attained, one specific factor in each of the socio-economic dynamics will be the primary focal point of the exposition: occupation. This is done for two reasons: First, given the number of factors, sub-factors, and interactions involved in the socio-economic dynamic, the presentation would quickly become complex and cumbersome; and second, occupation, of all the factors listed above, plays a central role in determining one's socio-economic position in society as will be explained in more detail below.

Dr. Alba Edwards, a noted Census Bureau expert on occupations and occupational classification over a half century ago wrote that, "…there is no other single characteristic that tells so much about a man and his status—social, intellectual, and economic—as does his occupation."[3] In quite specific terms he believed an individual's occupation would tell not only how he spends one half of his waking hours but also the manner of his life, that is, who he associates with, the kind of clothes he will wear, the kind of house he will live in, and even to some extent, the kind of food he eats, and to some degree, his cultural pursuits. Although Dr. Edwards' belief may be somewhat of an overstatement (given the passing of several decades and a sea change in American culture), there is still some basic truth in his words.

Perhaps the role of occupation in determining or influencing one's position in the income distribution, and specifically the middle class, has diminished over time, but it still retains a prominent position in the socio-economic dynamic. Simply consider how it continues to be closely related to the obvious factors like education, wealth, and income sources. Consequently, we will follow, primarily, the "occupation" characteristic over time in showing the relationship between a specific socio-economic dynamic and reaching a place in the middle class.

1870 to 1900

Toward the end of the nineteenth century, the middle class had been thought to be not much more than a sliver relative to what we think its size today.[4] It separated the working class, most of who by today's standard's were living in poverty, from the handful of wealthy capitalists, or owners of the banks, railroads, factories, and mines. This middle class was composed of a small group of managers and shop owners, assorted clerical, sales, and service workers, and farmers.

The occupational statistics from the Census Bureau contained in Table 5.2 give us a glimpse of this nascent middle class in 1900. Out of a total of 29 million persons in the civilian labor force at the turn of that century, approximately 18 percent were from the professional, managerial, clerical, and sales occupations, while the rest were in manual or trade occupations, service jobs, private household work, and occupations associated with farming. If one assumes that a small proportion of the 20 percent or so calling themselves farmers or farm managers in 1900

Table 5.2
Occupation Distribution of Workers, 1900, 1930, 1950, 1960, and 1970

Occupation	1970	1960	1950	1930	1900
Total Workers (in thousands)	79,802	67,990	58,999	48,686	29,030
Percent	100.0	100.0	100.0	100.0	100.0
White-Collar Workers	47.4	40.1	36.6	29.4	17.6
Prof., tech., and kindred	14.5	10.8	8.6	6.8	4.3
Managers, off'l., and prop.	8.1	8.1	8.7	7.4	5.8
Clerical	17.8	14.1	12.3	8.9	3.0
Sales	7.0	7.1	7.0	6.3	4.5
Manual and Service Workers	49.3	48.8	51.6	49.4	44.9
Craftsmen	13.9	13.6	14.2	12.8	10.5
Operatives	18.0	18.9	20.4	15.8	12.8
Laborers	4.7	5.2	6.6	10.6	12.5
Private hhld. workers	1.5	2.7	2.6	4.1	5.4
Service workers (n.e.c.)	11.3	8.5	7.9	5.7	3.6
Farm Workers	3.1	6.0	11.8	21.2	37.5
Farmers	1.8	3.7	7.4	12.4	19.9
Farm laborers	1.3	2.3	4.4	8.8	17.6

Source: U.S. Census Bureau   n.e.c. - Not elsewhere classified

were middle class as well, then America's middle class *was* indeed only a sliver of what we think of it today.

(Many Marxists view American society in this period as being comprised of workers, who only had their labor to sell, and a small collection of rich capitalists. The data here, as well as the research of others refute this notion. As shown above, nearly 20 percent of the labor force was composed of farmers, that is, "owners" of their own means of production in 1900.)

Economic differences in this middle class, no doubt, were not very large in terms of annual incomes or living conditions. Nor were demographic differences very large in terms of living arrangements and family sizes. Most people lived in married-couple families with two or three children and perhaps a grandparent or two. Public educational opportunities were taken advantage of to the same extent and, despite the cultural differences emanating from a variety of groups who had immigrated to this country in earlier years, this middle class adhered to accepted norms regarding leisure time (i.e., religious activities, recitals, amusement parks).

Becoming middle class via the socio-economic dynamic existing during the 1870 to 1900 period was driven largely by the early industrialization process and the desire to own one's means of livelihood, specifically, property, whether a small business or farm. Regarding the former, the story of America's industrialization has been told many times and in great detail. Spearheading the process, of course, was the expansion of railroads with miles and miles of railroad track constructed across the continent. Capital investment in factories was mushrooming during the period while iron ore and coal production was doubling. And new technologies like the telephone and telegraph were stitching the industrialization process together. The labor requirement for such a process not only involved manual workers, like miners, factory workers, and railroad men, but managers, conductors, clerks, and salesmen. But at the same time, the desire to be one's own boss, whether as a shopkeeper, mechanic, or journeyman of some kind, created a new class of small entrepreneurs, whose "ticket" into the middle class was simply the ownership of property. They joined millions of small farmers who owned their own means of production.

As much as today we hear about "education, education, education" as being the best bet for improving one's economic lot in life, 100 or so years ago that was not necessarily the case. The data charted in Figure 5.1 reveal that from 1870 to 1910, less than 10 percent of persons 17 years

Figure 5.1
Seventeen-Year-Olds - HS Grads.

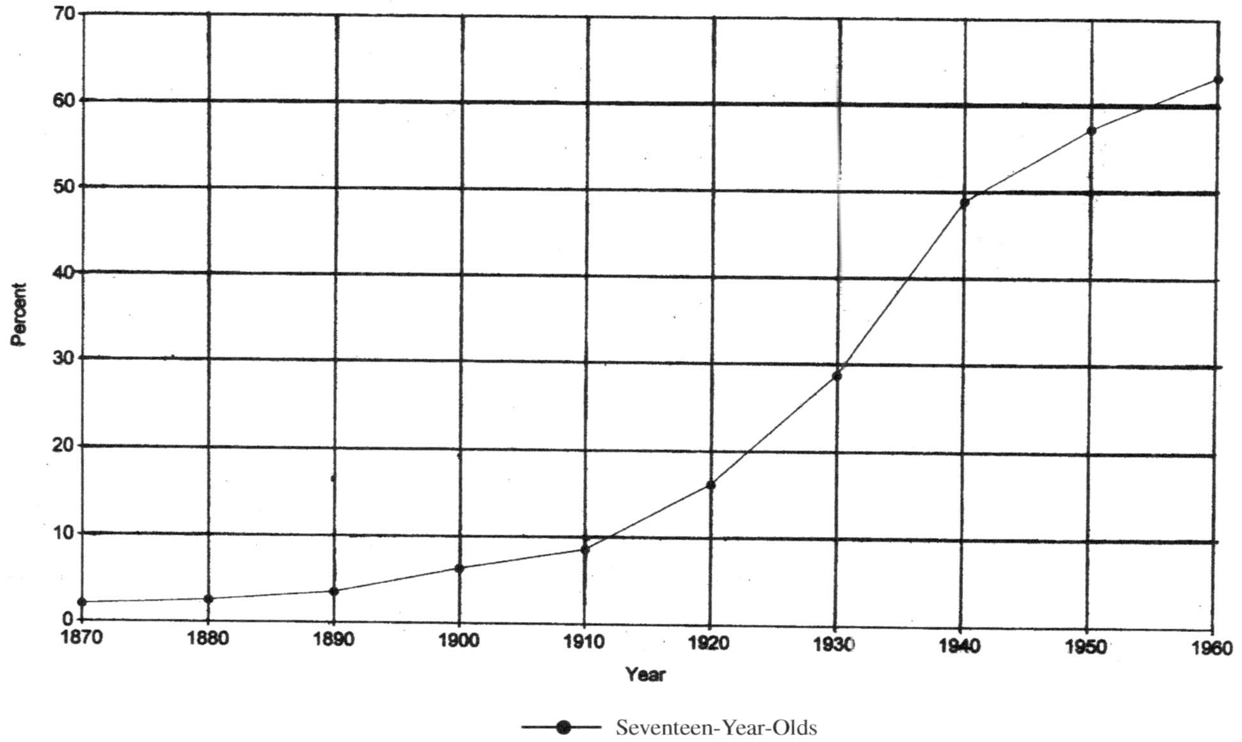

of age had a high school education. In other words, the adult work force during this period of our nation's history was not very educated.[5] Indeed, in 1870, 20 percent of the population age 10 or older was illiterate and by 1900 the comparable proportion had dropped only to 10 percent.[6]

Obviously, the elements of the socio-economic dynamic of the 1870 to 1900 period, which were important in the process of attaining a middle class life style, were relatively basic. In general, it required being a man, preferably married, who had moved into an occupation created as a result of the industrialization process or had accumulated some capital (wealth) and operated his own business or farm, and worked hard. To a lesser extent, it was probably a good idea that he was a citizen, in good health, went to church, and was a member of the white race. Rugged individualism was the key to upward socio-economic mobility in this period and perhaps this attribute of those attaining the ranks of the middle class were only emulating those above them—the so-called "robber barons."

1900 to 1930

America's industrialization process, of course, accelerated in the opening decades of the twentieth century—and our nation's cities filled. The nation's population grew from 76 million in 1900 to 123 million by 1930, and over 80 percent of the increase was in places considered to be urban (2,500 or more).[7] The great shift from an agricultural economy to an industrial economy was in full swing in this period, and the socio-economic dynamic began to reflect it, which would in turn have its impact on this nation's middle class.

The process of industrialization needed workers and, as is well-known, immigration was the answer. While approximately 3.7 million people immigrated into the country in the 1890 to 1899 period, in the next 10 year period it amounted to 8.2 million.[8] It was this surge in immigration that provided the workers for the packing plants, steel mills, and other goods-producing industries of the nation. The composition of the "working class" was now slowly changing.

This was the period in which the organized labor movement began to spread industrially. While trade unions, like the American Federation of Labor (AFL), had emerged during the 1880s, in certain industries, industrial unions were beginning to organize as the beginning of the next century drew near. For example, the United Mine Workers and the International Ladies Garment Workers Union had become powerful voices for the working class by 1900.

At the same time, the occupations associated with the middle class of earlier decades began to diversify and expand in specialties. Buyers, inspectors, purchasing agents, floormen, insurance and real estate agents, and various types of office occupations began to grow more common in businesses and companies. In manufacturing alone the number of managers, officials, and proprietors increased from 174,000 in 1900 to 406,000 by 1920.[9]

Coincident with the development of new occupations and work roles were the first indications of growing educational attainment. As shown in Figure 5.1, the proportion of 17 year olds who were high school graduates began to rise faster. By 1920 the proportion was up to 16 percent and by 1930 it was almost at 30 percent.[10] And in this period, college education became not just the privilege of the wealthy, but also one for the middle class, and in some rare instances, even the working class. While the number of persons with a Bachelor's degree grew from 9,400 to 27,400 between 1870 and 1900, over the next thirty years the number increased to 122,000.[11]

The nation's broad occupational structure was undergoing significant change in the 1900 to 1930 period reflecting the economy's shift away from agriculture and towards industry. As is shown in Table 5.2, the proportion of the nation's work force involved in farming and farming related occupations fell from 38 percent to only 21 percent between 1900 and 1930 while the proportion involved in manual and service related occupations rose from 45 to 49 percent. Furthermore, and very much related to the emerging middle class, was the growth in the proportion of persons working in white-collar occupations—from 18 to 29 percent.

The pace of economic activity over these 30 years was bumpy and irregular. Economic slowdowns and recessions, spurts of rapid economic growth, a world war, and labor union strife all punctuated this period. But the lot of the working man slowly improved. His annual average earnings (in 1914 dollars) rose from $445 in 1900 to $725 by 1930.[12] These gains in the real earnings of workers helped more and more families rise up out of poverty and move further up in the income distribution. While the ratio of the average annual earnings of workers to the poverty line in 1905 was 1.092 (or average earnings were 9.2 percent above the poverty level) by 1925 the ratio was 1.146 (or 14.6 percent above the poverty level).[13]

These economic developments had a profound impact on the nation's working class and middle class as it stood on the doorstep of the Great Depression. Not only had both groups increased in number but their economic lots in life had improved markedly. A significant part of the working class was able to move out of poverty while the middle class's discretionary income had grown significantly.

The critical elements of the nation's socio-economic dynamic for attaining a middle class life style had changed significantly. "Wage" jobs became more common and these tended to be found in the towns and cities of the industrializing nation. While having a good job was a key, it was especially important if the job was in the white-collar occupations and in a nonagricultural industry like banking or finance. A high school education became more important in many of these jobs. But even certain manual and service occupations would put one into the middle class, especially if it was a labor union job and one requiring a certain amount of skill. Race, unfortunately, continued to be a liability but ethnicity grew of less importance because of the vast number of immigrants who had arrived in the country. And the middle class of this period was still reserved primarily for the married-couple families.

This change in the socio-economic dynamic also produced a phenomenon that would become even more evident in latter years. The lines between the middle class and the working class as defined at the turn of the century had begun to blur over this 30-year period and especially so during the 1920s. The reason: Consumerism. With more money coming into working families, the opportunity to spend on goods and services of all kinds had arrived. Automobiles, radios, motion pictures, and other "things" that only the rich could afford were now becoming available to those in the middle class—and even the working class. And assisting this surge in wants was the availability of installment credit. Between 1919 and 1929, the level of installment credit had mushroomed from $800 million to $3.5 billion (in nominal dollars).[14] This "blurring" of class lines, however, was put on hold for a while as the nation's socio-economic dynamic began another redefinition in the 1930s.

1930 to 1955

The Great Depression had a profound impact on the nation's income distribution. Its gradual shift upwards, reflecting the rise of the working class into the middle class, came to a halt. Among the rich and wealthy, some fortunes slowly melted away and for others they suddenly collapsed. The great "compression" of the income distribution had begun.

The causes of the depression have been long debated. Stock market and real estate speculation, the international drop in commodity prices, the overextension of installment credit, and other economic problems, all came crashing down upon the American economy like a big ocean wave. Business failures rose, unemployment skyrocketed, and the real annual earnings of employees were cut by a third between 1929 and 1933.[15] Consumption expenditures were slashed and the newly found pool of money for discretionary purchases by the middle class dried up. The exit out of poverty for many from the working class now reversed itself. The poverty rate rose during the early 1930s and by mid-decade was estimated to be anywhere from 45 to 63 percent of the population.[16]

So, the evolving middle class was dealt a blow, but a blow from which it would take stock, regroup, and then try to move forward again. As students of this era know, this was a time of social rethinking. American capitalism had been brought into question, and many from the working class and middle class now reached out for help. With the passage of such Federal legislation as the Norris-LaGuardia Act, the Industrial Recovery Act, and the National Labor Relations Act, the labor union movement gained new momentum and spread ever deeper into the nation's industrial sector. Union membership more than doubled between 1935 and 1940 and its share of nonagricultural employment rose from 13 to 27 percent.[17]

With the beginning of the 1940s and WWII, the nation's income distribution entered another phase of the great "compression"—it began shifting upwards again. Mobilization for war had a profound impact on the nation's labor force and society. The demand for all kinds of labor surged and unemployment shriveled driving real wages higher. Additional help in raising wages, especially for those in the lower skilled occupations, was the new social legislation relating to the minimum wage and the bargaining power of organized labor. Another significant labor force development sparked by the war was the increase in labor force participation of women—a development which had major significance in the emerging socio-economic dynamic of this period.

The social disruption caused by the Great Depression and WWII not only led to a more compressed income distribution, it led to a further blurring of the class lines between the working class and middle class. One reason this happened was that all through these years Americans were becoming better and better educated. As shown in Figure 5.1, the percent of persons age 17 who were high school graduates had almost doubled between 1930 and 1950 jumping from about 29 percent to 57 percent. At the same time, the number of persons receiving degrees from colleges and universities simply exploded between 1930 and 1950. While in 1930 about 140,000 degrees were conferred, by 1950 the comparable number approached 500,000.[18]

The country's investment in human capital, the changes that had taken place in the nation's industrial sector as a result of WWII, and the new social legislation enacted during the Great Depression, all had significant repercussions for the middle class by the decade of the 1950s. This can be seen by simply looking at the occupational structures of the work force as of 1930 and 1950, which are shown in Table 5.2. Greater proportions of workers by the mid-century mark were now working in white-collar occupations than in 1930—37 percent vs. 29 percent. Even in the higher skilled blue-collar occupations—the craftsmen and operative jobs—the proportions rose from 28 to 34 percent. This occupational restructuring, of course, was taking place at the expense of farmers and farm workers who went from representing 21 percent of all workers in 1930 to only 12 percent by 1950. Although the manual and service occupations still were the predominant occupation group in the economy, it would only be a few years until white collar occupations took their place.[19] Indeed, if one assumes that employment in white collar occupations was synonymous with middle class status, and that even a small proportion of farmers and those in manual occupations could be considered in the middle class, this segment of society, that had once been a "sliver," was now a significant "wedge" of the population.

It would not be hyperbole to say that the tectonic plates beneath the nation's socio-economic dynamic had undergone cataclysmic shifts between 1930 and 1955. When examining all the socio-economic classes—from lower to upper—virtually all of the elements in the socio-economic dynamic took on more significance and less significance at one time or another during the period. For attaining a position in the middle class it was not only important to hold a job, but education and skill became increasingly important as did the industry and occupation in which one worked. But it was less important to be a white, Anglo-Saxon, Protestant, or from a married couple family, or a citizen who borrowed books from the library. The role of the Federal government, for the first time, grew more important for helping to reach (or stay in) the middle class—from providing unemployment insurance to offering the GI Bill to veterans in the 1950s.

This transformation of the class structure, especially in the working class and middle class, had a gradual homogenizing effect. This could be seen everywhere in the early 1950s, from the rows and rows of tract housing that sprang up in the suburbs of the nation to the consumption items that these classes spent their paychecks on, like Fords, Chevrolets, and Plymouths. For some sociologists of that time, this transformation was ominous. C. Wright Mills wrote about the changes that had taken place between the "old" middle class of the late nineteenth century and the "new" middle class that had emerged by mid-twentieth century. In his book, *White Collar*, he lamented the loss of the farmers, small merchants, and manufacturers who were anchored to their property only to be replaced by the millions of managers, teachers, office workers, salespersons, clerks, insurance agents, and lawyers who were now merely "wage" workers employed by corporate giants and commercial enterprises.[20] This new middle class was suffering from a malaise, he suggested, because it was now simply at the "beck and call" of an impersonal employer. He wrote the following indictment:

> Newly created in a harsh time of creation, white-collar man has no culture to lean upon except the contents of a mass society that has shaped him and seeks to manipulate him to its alien ends.[21]

Unfortunately, C. Wright Mills died in 1962, never to witness the *second* middle class revolution that was only a few decades away.

1955 to 1975

The great compression of the income distribution, which had taken place between 1930 and 1955, was followed by its uniform expansion—that is, everyone's income rose. In consequence, the nation's poverty rate fell from 22 percent in 1959 to 12 percent by 1975.[22] The income gap reached its narrowest point of the century in the mid-1960s. The middle class was now solidly entrenched in American society; approximately 53 percent of all households had annual incomes (in 2006 dollars) between $25,000 and $75,000 by 1975.[23] New automobiles, new houses, and many consumer durables, like color televisions, stereophonic equipment, and touch-tone telephones, now became necessities for millions of middle class consumers.

Despite the upward shifting of the income distribution, however, the social scene had become chaotic. Race riots in our biggest cities, political assassinations, an unpopular war in Vietnam, all of these tore at the nation's social fabric. Many of the nation's youths went off marching to another drummer that their parents didn't understand, challenging their way of life. A President resigned in disgrace and political acrimony scorched the body politic. While the middle class was enjoying its material well-being, it was also looking deep inside itself and wondering what had happened to the "happy America" of the 1950s.

Subtle changes were also beginning to be observed in this period to the most revered American institution of all—the family. Married-couple families, although still the dominant type of household in society, were beginning to lose ground to "nonfamily" households and single-parent families. The maturing of the baby boom generation, of course, contributed to this development as did the rising divorce rate and incidence of children born out of wedlock. Such changes signaled the start of new shifts in the nation's socio-economic dynamic.

One of the repercussions of these changes, as well other social changes taking place in society, was the increased labor force activity on the part of women. Women, of course, had played a crucial role in the nation's work force during WWII but many presumed that that was a temporary phenomenon. By the mid-1950s, however, labor force participation rates of women began rising again: in 1955 the rate for women age 25 to 54 was about 40 percent and in 1965 it was 45 percent. And it didn't stop rising. By 1975, 56 percent of all women in this age group were in the nation's work force.[24]

Women were providing the labor supply for a growing economy, especially in the area of white-collar work. Between 1950 and 1970 the number of women employed had increased by almost 14 million—and 72 percent of this growth took place in professional, managerial, clerical, and sales occupations.[25] The world of work—and the face of the worker—had changed significantly since the Great Depression.

The supply of college-educated workers was also beginning to increase more rapidly during this period as the baby boom generation, or that part of it that went on to higher education, graduated and entered the work force. Indeed, between 1955 and 1970, the number of bachelors, masters, and Ph.D. degrees that were conferred had tripled and topped the 1 million mark at the beginning of the 1970s.[26] Economists who studied the "economic return to schooling" found that the returns had indeed increased during the 1960s only to fall back in the 1970s as the labor markets became inundated with educated young people.[27]

The industrialization process in the nation was beginning to slow down during these years as the nation's economic base began shifting in earnest from a goods-producer to a service-producer. While employment in manufacturing continued to grow, jobs in the nation's service sector were skyrocketing. Between 1955 and 1975, the number of payroll jobs in the service-producing sector of the economy jumped from 32 million to 56 million, and by the end of that period accounted for 3 out of every 4 jobs.[28] Jobs in the health, education, and financial service industries were providing employment for the millions of new college graduates and married women coming into the labor force. This shifting of jobs from the "old-line" goods-producing sector to the "hot" new industries in the service-producing sector was only the beginning of much larger shifts to take place in the nation's industrial structure in the years to come.

Reflecting the industrial shifts occurring during the 1955 to 1975 period, was the further employment growth in white-collar occupations and the relative decline in blue-collar and farm occupations, especially the ones requiring the least skills and education. Table 5.2 depicts these shifts between 1950 and 1970. Employment in professional and clerical occupations, which accounted for 1 out of 5 workers in 1950 had moved up to account for almost 1 out of every 3 workers. Blue-collar and farm laborers accounted for only 6 percent of total employment in 1970 but 20 years earlier it was 11 percent. Clearly, a skilled-biased occupational shift was well underway.

Reaching the middle class during these years certainly required good job skills and the more education the better. This was especially the case if one was not from a married-couple family. Weakening family ties imperiled single-parent mothers, and in particular those who were black and living in the nation's inner cities. Low-wage jobs were also becoming more common with the explosion in "fast food" restaurants and other service establishments. Of course, this was the era of the "Great Society" in which the Federal government had supposedly strengthened the social safety net—and, indeed, it no doubt helped some families and individuals retain their middle class status. Medicare, introduced in 1965, for example, eased the medical expenses for many elderly middle-class households. The upheaval among blacks in the quest for their civil rights would eventually make it that much easier for millions of them to reach the middle class, and stay there.

1975 to 2000

It was during the closing decades of the last century that the "morphing" of the American middle class truly got underway. By the year 2000, this process had produced a segment of society that was as broad and heterogeneous as its counterpart was narrow and homogeneous in the year 1900.

The economic history of this period is relatively familiar and the developments with respect to income inequality were covered in Chapter 2. As was discussed there, the trend in real incomes of American families had slowed significantly beginning in the 1970s relative to what had taken place in earlier post-WWII years. Accompanying that event was the increase in wage and earnings inequality. For some economists, this was convincing evidence that the demand for labor had indeed become truly "skill-biased"—and the beginning of another change in the nation's socio-economic dynamic was taking place.

The wage and earnings developments in the labor market, of course, worked their way into the nation's income distribution. Income inequality began rising as the incomes in the upper half of the income distribution began outpacing those in the lower half, at least until the mid-1990s. The income distribution "escalators" had now become clearly marked: "Up" for the educated and skilled and "Down" for the poorly educated and unskilled.

In addition, other developments were taking place that would have profound effects on society and becoming middle class. The first was the role of the computer and the advent of the information age, the second was the opening of world-wide trading markets (i.e., globalization), and the third was the unrelenting expansion of consumerism, or as some might call it, "the quest for more."

Information technology, of course, blossomed in the closing decades of the twentieth century and it had a profound impact on the economic structure of the nation. Advances in computers and telecommunications transformed the way the economy operated. Everything from keeping track of inventories to the billing of customers to advertising products became involved with computers. Manufacturing processes became "computerized" and financial services once requiring person-to-person interchanges were handled via computers. Electronic data files relating to customers, products, and markets could be instantaneously moved about the country via the Internet. The economic efficiencies of the computer revolution came fast and furious and their potential appeared, and still appear, unlimited.

New industries were established. By the year 2000, almost 2 million workers were employed in the computer and data processing services industry alone.[29] Not only had new industries developed as a result of the computer revolution, but by the end of the century computer technology had changed the way businesses and commerce was transacted and the way the national economy operated. Just as railroads and electricity had sparked the transition from an agricultural economy to an industrial one in the nineteenth century, the computer revolution had launched the U.S. economy into the information age.

New occupations necessary for such an economic transformation, of course, were required, just as they were 100 years or so ago in the transition from an agricultural to industrial economy. But these new occupations were considerably more difficult to classify as either blue-collar or white-collar occupations. Some of these new positions required high levels of education and others only a basic familiarity with a computer keyboard. Names of occupations associated with the beginnings of the computer revolution, like programmer and systems analyst, have been added to in bewildering abundance. Computer security specialist, webmaster, database administrator, and data communications analyst are only a few of the many new occupations associated with the ever expanding information age.

It was not as if old line industries like manufacturing, construction, and mining had died and gone away. Indeed, by the year 2000 these three "goods-producers" still accounted for 1 out of every 5 nonfarm jobs in the nation.[30] But many of these jobs also had been touched by the computer revolution. Because of this radical transformation in the world of work that had its beginnings in the 1970s, as well as other changes that had taken place in the work force, the nation developed a new occupational classification system. The white-collar and blue-collar labels that had identified peoples' jobs for years were set aside for a more "up-to-date" classification scheme.[31] Table 5.3 presents this new classification for the years 1983 and 2002 based on the occupations persons were employed in each of those years.

Managerial and professional specialty occupations and technical, sales, and administrative support occupations accounted for 54 percent of all workers in 1983 and by 2002 almost 60 percent. These occupations are similar to what had been referred to earlier as the white-collar occupations. This segment's representation in the nation's occupational structure had tripled over the last 100 years or so—from 20 percent (Table 5.2) to 60 percent (Table 5.3).

Three of the fastest growing occupation groups among professional specialty occupations were in the fields of health (assessment and treating occupations), education (teachers) and computers (systems analysts and scientists). Those employed in the last occupation group alone grew from 276,000 to 1.7 million.

In contrast to this rapid expansion was the more moderate growth of workers in technical, sales, and administrative support occupations. But the overall proportions are deceptive. Large employment increases were observed in the occupation of health technician and technologist, sales representative in finance and business services, and insurance adjuster and investigator.

Table 5.3
Occupation Distribution of Employed Workers, 1983 and 2002

Occupation	2002	1983
Total Workers (in thousands)	136,485	100,834
Percent	100.0	100.0
Managerial and Professional Specialty	31.1	23.4
Executive, administrative, managerial	14.9	10.7
Professional specialty	16.1	12.7
Computer systems analyst	1.3	0.3
Technical, Sales, Administrative Support	28.5	31.0
Technicians and related support	3.3	3.0
Sales	11.9	11.7
Service	14.1	13.7
Protective service	1.9	1.7
Precision, Production, Craft, Repair	10.7	12.2
Operators, Fabricators, Laborers	13.0	16.0
Machine operators, assemblers	4.8	7.7
Farming, forestry, fishing	2.5	3.7

Source: U.S. Census Bureau

The old blue-collar occupation categories, now considered to be composed of "precision production, craft, and repair" occupations and "operators, fabricators, and laborers" continued to lose their relative importance among all occupations. Their proportion of total employment in 1983 was 28 percent and in 2002 only 24 percent. But here also, occupations requiring knowledge of computers advanced in size (e.g., data processing equipment repairers).

In short, occupations in which work activities could be aided by the computer might either jeopardize or enhance employment opportunities. Examples of the former were the occupations found in the area of financial record processing and examples of the latter were such specific occupations like cashier and shipping and receiving clerk. But the bottom line was that the higher the education or skill level required in doing the work of a specific occupation, the greater the necessity for knowing something about computers. Again, this was a very significant change in the nation's socio-economic dynamic.

The second additional development that had a profound effect on society and one's chances of making it into the middle class and staying there in the 1975 to 2000 period was the role of "globalization." The conjoining of advances in telecommunication and transportation, with other changes (e.g., the spread of political freedom and democracy) in recent decades has fostered a new era of world trade.

Much has been made of globalization and its economic consequences for Americans, as well as other nations. Indeed, it has been argued that globalization has resulted in job loss for many of our workers in various industries and occupations and led to a wider income gap—and weakened the middle class. On the other hand, some of the benefits of open foreign markets have included cheaper consumer prices and greater economic efficiencies at home. Nevertheless, with the recent passage of CAFTA (Central American Free Trade Agreement), along with NAFTA (North American Free Trade Agreement) and the other trading agreements worked out in recent years, it is evident that the globalization process will continue.

Obviously, American jobs have been "outsourced" to cheaper labor markets in China, India, Mexico, and elsewhere, and many of these jobs involved "modern day" skills and know how. But the trade-offs in the form of the overall economic benefits to society must be considered. Naturally, the TV-news film footage of a computer programmer going home to tell his wife that his job has been outsourced to India resonates more with the masses than the fact that his company will now be more competitive and produce their products for lower consumer prices. But the key point for the new socio-economic dynamic that evolved in the 1975 to 2000 period was simple: Get all the education and training you can—in an occupation in demand!

The Bureau of Labor Statistics (BLS) publishes occupational information and occupational employment projections on a regular basis. In 2001, the agency released a list of what will be the fastest growing occupations between 2000 and 2010. Out of the 30 listed, 10 were associated with computers and 8 required a Bachelor's degree or better.[32] Many of the other occupations, no doubt, involved computer "know how."

The third and last development in the 1975 to 2000 period that impacted the socio-economic dynamic of these years was the explosion in consumerism. Ever since the end of WWII and the end of restrictions on consumption, the nation's taste for spending on all sorts of consumer goods grew enormously. For example, by 1955 each American was spending $8,383 a year (in 2000 dollars) on consumer goods of all kinds and by 1975 the comparable figure reached $13,320 a year. But then the real explosion in "the need for more" really took off and by the opening of the new century, per capita consumption, in inflation adjusted dollars, totaled $23,862.[33]

Clearly, the middle class was growing throughout this period (despite some in the elite media who believed otherwise). Real household incomes, although not growing uniformly across the income distribution, were nevertheless growing and fueling the urge to spend money on consumer goods and services of all kinds. Indeed, a significant portion of the middle class was most likely over-spending. The nation's saving rate, which was 7 percent in 1955 and almost 11 percent in 1975, slowly declined thereafter and then plummeted in the late 1990s and approached the 2 percent level by 2000.[34] For many households, middle class life styles were being acquired via a credit card.

In conclusion, the tectonic plates underlying the nation's socio-economic dynamic shifted mightily in the last quarter of the twentieth century—perhaps more so than in any other period—resulting in a "morphing" of America's middle class. Once thought to be the domain of white-collar workers and a few highly skilled blue-collar workers, the middle class had been transformed into a highly diverse and heterogeneous agglomeration of families and households. Economic, social, and demographic factors had come together in such a way as to redefine it.

"Morphing" and the Second Middle Class Revolution

As the nation entered the new millennium, the middle class in America had reached its greatest size in the nation's history. According to the Census Bureau's decennial census, in 1999, 72.5 million households had annual incomes that ranged from $25,000 to $150,000.[35]

By the year 2000, an immigrant taxicab driver and a Harvard-educated lawyer could both sit down in a Starbuck's, get on their laptop computers or cell phones, and buy consumer products from eBay or Amazon.com and check out the status of their 401(k)s—and both think of themselves as middle class. Being a black or Hispanic or single parent no longer relegated you to the "other side of the tracks" or the "projects." You didn't necessarily have to be a "church-goer" or wear a tie to work to be thought of as middle class. You could drive a Mercedes to the office or you could take a bus; you could drive a truck to the factory or you could take your Cadillac. Some white-collar workers now wore Polo shirts to work and some blue-collar workers wore ties.

As one sociologist observed at the close of the twentieth century, the "…relationship between the distribution of income and the class structure is clear at the extremes but somewhat blurred in the middle."[36] The term "somewhat" can only be considered an understatement after reviewing the socio-economic dynamic of the 1975-2000 period. This blurring the sociologist referred to was, quite simply, the result of the "morphing" of the nation's middle class.

Figures 5.2a and 5.2b compare and contrast both the first *and* second middle class revolutions that took place in the last century. The upper panel, Figure 5.2a, depicts what happened to the nation's income distribution between 1929 and 1959—when the middle class truly emerged.[37] While defining the middle class in both years has been intentionally avoided, one can certainly obtain some sense of what may have happened to it by simply looking at the middle of the income distributions depicted in the graphs for those years. We know that in 1929, the approximate amount of income required for a minimally adequate level of living was slightly less than $2,500 (in 1962 dollars) for a family of four persons.[38] This implies that a significant proportion of the nation's population (somewhere in the neighborhood of one third) was living in poverty. Given the nature of the income distribution at that time, this meant the middle class (however defined in terms of income) was not very large. By 1959, however, the distribution flattened out as a result of rising real incomes, and the middle class had mushroomed as a consequence. Relative to the income distribution in 1929, the middle of the income distribution in 1959 "thickened" considerably. One can sense this thickening also by the increase in the real average annual incomes over these years—from $4,123 to $6,865. Although official government poverty thresholds had not been established by 1959, the comparable poverty line in 1959 was probably about $3,000 (in 1962 dollars).[39]

A depiction of the second middle class revolution is displayed in the lower panel of Figure 5.2b. At first glance the differences in the two graphs do not appear as great as those depicted in the upper panel for 1929 and 1959 (both the graph for 1969 and 1999 are drawn in terms of 2003 dollars so as to adjust for the effects of inflation). Nevertheless, upon closer examination significant differences can be seen in the nation's income distribution between 1969 and 1999.

Unlike in the upper panel where the focus of attention was on the thickening in the middle of the income distribution, in the lower panel attention should be focused on the thickening in the upper tail of the 1999 distribution relative to that in 1969. Households with annual incomes of $75,000 or more increased their representation dramatically—from 10 percent to 26 percent. And while this includes the increase in the

Figure 5.2a
Households by Income
1929 and 1959 (in 1962 dollars)

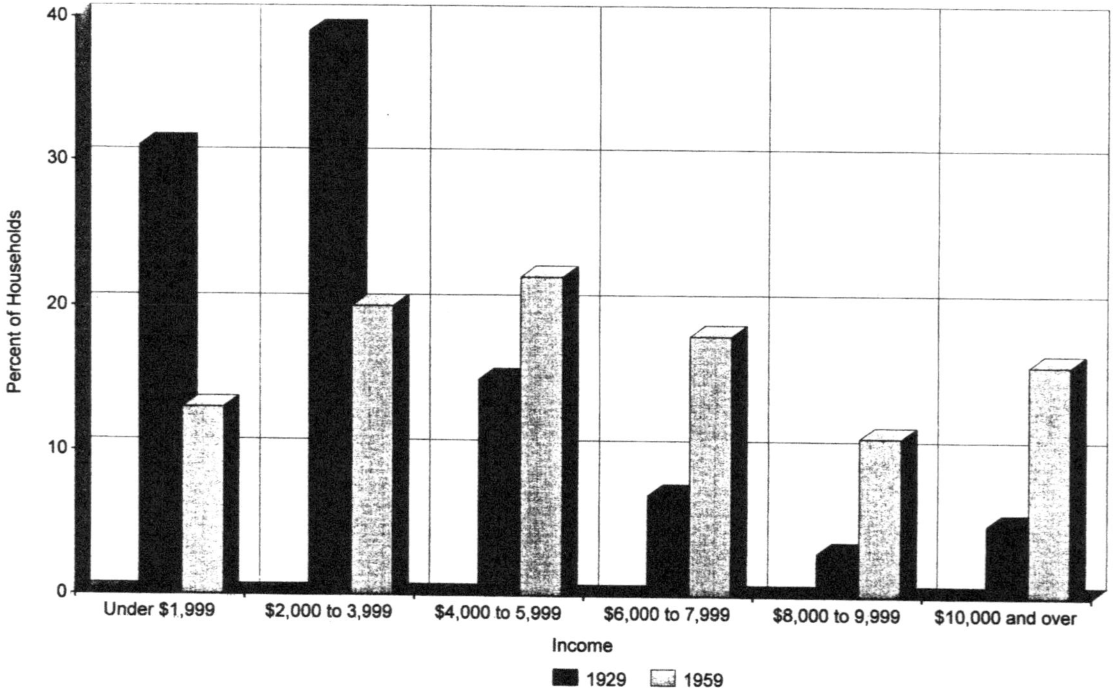

Figure 5.2b
Households by Income
1969 and 1999 (in 2003 dollars)

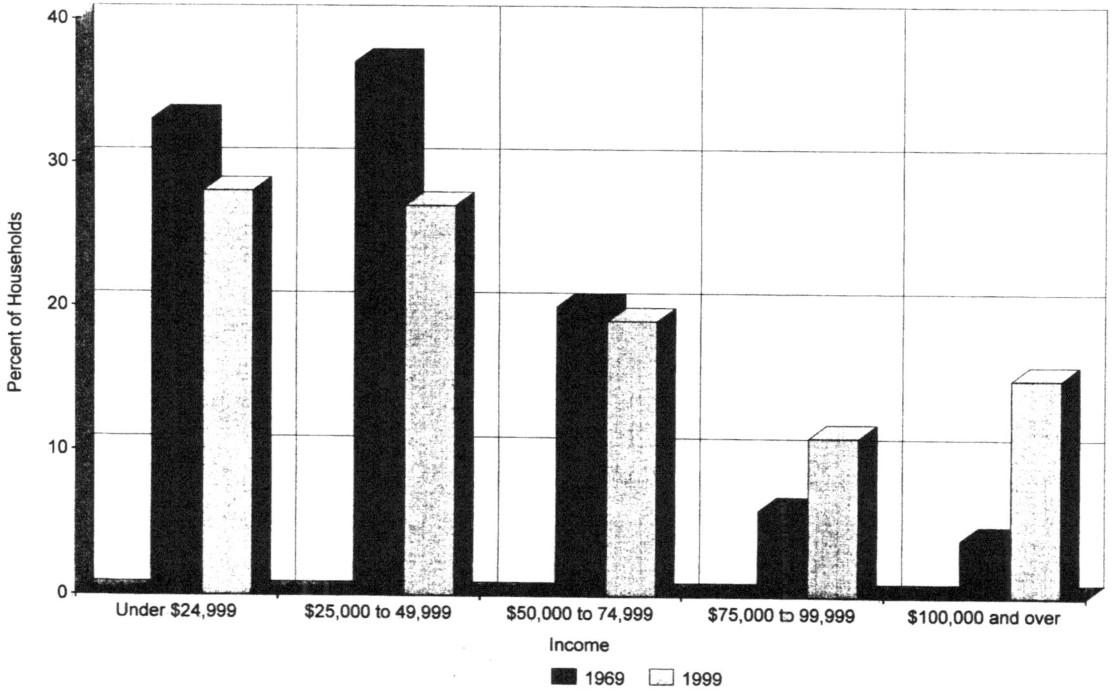

proportion of households with incomes of $150,000 or more, there is no doubt that the bulk of the thickening was due to households with incomes moving into the $75,000 to $149,999 range. In short, millions of middle class American families during the 1969 to 1999 period were receiving annual incomes—for whatever the reasons—that were now in the six digit category, when only thirty years ago this possibility was just a "pipedream."

The reason for the second middle class revolution, just as in the case of the first, can be found in the socio-economic dynamic of the period. But the changes in the dynamic between 1975 and 2000 were simply much more profound and complex than the changes that had taken place in the dynamics of the earlier periods.

Basically, the operation of any period's socio-economic dynamic can be thought of as the interactive process between society's economic factors and its social factors (and here, demographic factors such as family composition, marital status, education and so on, are considered as a part of the social factors). Some of the major factors in the dynamics were displayed in Table 5.1. During each period, these social and economic factors are acting and interacting—and influencing society's decision making.

Indeed, this interactive process can be considered the mechanism of social enculturation, in other words, how a society becomes what it is. The process is dynamic. Economic forces interact with social forces, which in turn influence the economic forces, and this process produces the society—along with its income distribution—that we become a part of. Critical to understanding the process is its origination in this country.

The founding fathers of this nation, and their ancestors, advanced beliefs in certain concepts, such as, a concept of freedom, a concept of laws, a concept of property. These concepts were set down in a place with bountiful resources. The creation of wealth was the natural consequence of these concepts and production and consumption was their offspring. The process of production and consumption, or economic factors, influenced the social factors and, ultimately, the society. The nation was initially agrarian in nature. Agricultural production created wealth and to produce more wealth required more resources, including more people. Not only do we find the "peculiar institution," or slavery, emerging as a part of the culture, but also "peoples" of different tongues and nationalities coming to the nation's shores.

In the early nineteenth century, the nation's socio-economic dynamic was very basic: work (mostly agricultural), family (mostly married couples), culture (mostly religion). But slowly, with the development of various technologies, more capital, more education and other "enablers," the socio-economic dynamic began to enlarge—in other words, the socio-economic dynamic began to change. The greatest social upheaval in the nation's history took place in the mid-nineteenth century—the Civil War—and the enculturation process was greatly impacted upon. In consequence, the social factors that now affected the creation of wealth through the twin processes of production and consumption changed as well.

One hundred and fifty years later, the socio-economic dynamic is much more complicated and much larger simply because of the passage of time. And it became more complicated and larger at a faster rate in the latter part of the twentieth century than any other time in the past century. And *this* is what led to the morphing of the middle class and its second revolution.

The economic factors by 1975 were to experience profound change, not only in the context of production and consumption, but in what was *enabling* them to change. One of these enablers was the growth in the incomes of the middle class, in real (inflation adjusted) terms. They had grown to such an extent since the early part of the century, that poverty, as it was experienced back then, was no longer an issue. The vast majority of the middle class were now free to spend and consume.

So it was "consumerism" that was the great unifier of the expanding middle class in the closing decades of the twentieth century, and income growth, one of the enablers. By 2000, the black family in rural Georgia could have a 40-inch flat screen television set just like the white suburban family in Westchester County, New York, and both of them could have Internet access. Perhaps their incomes were vastly different (maybe $40,000 a year versus $140,000) and their cultural interests and religious affiliations were very different, but both households still considered themselves to be members of this country's middle class.

Other "enablers" that helped to make this modern-day consumerism possible was technology and education. The technological advances in telecommunications and computers, for example, revolutionized how people communicated with each other and how commerce was conducted. With the year-by-year improvements in these new technologies, their prices dropped further and further making them more affordable for families and households further down the income ladder. The ubiquitous cell phone, for example, is now used by virtually everyone across the income distribution. Digital cameras, DVD players, and iPods became the "gadgetry du jour" for the middle class kids whether they were from

Hoboken, New Jersey or Henrietta, Texas. Because of the ever-changing technology in the semi-conductor (i.e., chips) field, the price of last year's technology, which was affordable by only a few, was now available to the masses.[40]

In some respects, the same was true in the travel and transportation industry. Prices have increased, obviously, but not as much as the overall cost of living. Caribbean cruises, once the luxury of the rich, became commonplace for the middle class, and weekend getaways to Las Vegas, Atlantic City, and Foxwoods were tailor-made with the middle-class pocketbook in mind.

Because educational attainment in present-day America has reached such heights (9 out of every 10 employed persons in 2003 had at least a high school diploma), information in society is absorbed like a sponge. Assisting in this consumption of information, of course, has been the Internet. By 2003, approximately 166 million people 18 years of age or over had access to the Internet either at home, work, or some other way—and the vast middle class was the chief consumer. Roughly 52 percent of the 166 million Internet users were individuals from households in the income range of $50,000 to $150,000 a year.[41] The exposure to information of all kinds acts as a fuel for consumerism. Whatever one's reason for "surfing the net," the open window on the world had boosted consumption in the final analysis—and assisted in the "morphing" of the middle class.

"Gloomers and Doomers"

For whatever the reason or reasons, the conception of America's middle class has often troubled some observers of the nation's social scene. It may be because of its linkage to the Marxian concept of the bourgeoisie, or the upper middle class and the quasi-property owners. There is that feeling expressed in many of these observers' writings that this class's economic success is purely temporal and not really earned—a class of society not knowing what it is all about. At the same time, there is this sentiment or pathos expressed for the class below, the working class or the working poor, or simply the poor and those who have been swept aside by the forward movement of the economy.

Beginning with Thorstein Veblen at the end of the nineteenth and beginning of the twentieth century, the economic transformation of the nation (e.g., from agriculture to industry) has always had a profound affect upon the thinking and views of intellectuals regarding the country's social structure. In Veblen's *Theory of the Leisure Class* he discusses the inefficiencies of "conspicuous consumption" and its widespread occurrence across the class structure.[42] The middle class, as he saw it in his time, was unduly concerned with keeping up appearances for the sake of sustaining their own self-respect and dignity. The economic gains of this growing "sliver" of society (i.e., the middle class) for Veblen, in many respects, were simply signs of ostentation.

By mid-twentieth century, as the nation's industrial economy grew and became more developed and the white-collar work force became synonymous with the middle class, other observers raised the "red flags" of danger about this growing segment of society. As was mentioned earlier, according to the views of C. Wright Mills this "new" middle class had actually become rudderless by the 1950s.[43] They worked for wages and salaries, paid by invisible corporate enterprises, and were vastly different from the middle class of the late nineteenth and early twentieth centuries—the age of the small farmers and shopkeepers who were tied to physical pieces of property. To Mills this new white-collar segment of society was in a malaise, duped by the impersonal corporate giants that the American economy had bred. Again, despite a segment of society that had gone through a cataclysmic economic depression and worldwide war and found its economic footing and were now buying new cars, refrigerators, and homes in booming suburban neighborhoods, the bells of doom were pealing.

Moving ahead another thirty or forty years, the cries of middle class disaster were heard again from some of the nation's social observers. In the 1980s, of course, there was the announcement of the "decline of the middle class" associated with the deindustrialization and downsizing of America—the echoes of which can still be heard to this day. [44] In the following decades, the demise of the middle class was upon the nation *again,* this time because of globalization and outsourcing and the movement of the economy into the "information age." Indeed, in the Presidential election of 2004 a "Middle Class Misery Index" was ballyhooed by the Democratic presidential hopeful Senator John Kerry, an index presumably indicating how economically battered the middle class really was.[45]

One book that stands out as pealing the death knell for the middle class in recent decades is entitled, *Fear of Falling* by Barbara Ehrenreich.[46] (This book should not be confused with her later books about low-wage workers, *Nickel and Dimed,* and unemployed white-collar workers, *Bait and Switch.*) It stands out because it harkens back to the days of C. Wright Mills who worried about the fact that the "new" middle class were simply "wage and salary slaves" to big business. Ehrenreich focuses in on only a part of today's middle class, the professional middle class whose status in society is based only on education and not capital nor property. Despite their economic success, she believes they live in peril of losing their jobs—and their middle class status. Once again, it is the distant drum of economic change (i.e., technological change, shifting trade patterns) that presumably threatens the economic lives of this professional middle class.

There are many other contemporary tomes in the bookstores about the trials and travails of the American middle class. Some discuss the problems of low-wage workers and two-income households and others describe the treadmill breadwinners are on and yet others lament the lack of quality family time as a result of simply keeping the family afloat. It is all part of the new middle class "squeeze" genre.

For these writers and intellectuals who only see a middle class in trouble, the problem is they have never, first, really understood this country's process of upward economic mobility, and second, they have never given up on what they think is "good" economically for society. They distrust the free market, capitalistic system the nation was built upon; they only decry the plight of the working class and the poor and pick away at the economic success of the middle class.

As will be shown in the next chapter, the morphing of the middle class in this nation in recent years entailed not only a sudden expansion of its upper tier but also the gradual assimilation of this country's working class. This was never supposed to happen—at least according to the "gloomers and doomers!"

Notes

1.   The term "melting pot" is believed to have originated from the play, *The Melting Pot*, by Israel Zangwill (1864-1926), a British-born Zionist. The play was first performed in Washington, DC in 1908.
2.   The term, socio-economic dynamic, is shorthand for referring to the process in which social, economic, and demographic factors in life influence our choices and decision- making. Demographic factors, therefore, are subsumed to reside under the term "socio." See Appendix B for a conceptual discussion.
3.   Alba Edwards, *Comparative Occupation Statistics for the United States, 1870 to 1940*, Sixteenth Census of the Population (Washington, DC: Department of Commerce, Bureau of the Census, 1943).
4.   One observer speculated that it represented at best only 20 percent of society. See, Fred Pfeil, "Class," *Encyclopedia of American Cultural and Intellectual History* (New York: Charles Scribner's Sons, 2001), Vol. 3, pp. 131-138.
5.   U.S. Bureau of the Census, *Historical Statistics of the United States: Colonial Times to 1970, Part 1,* (Washington, DC: USGPO, 1975), Series H 599, p. 379.

6.   *Ibid.*, Series H 664, p. 382.
7.   *Ibid.*, Series A 57 and A 69, p. 11.
8.   *Ibid.*, Series C 89, pp. 105-106.
9.   *Ibid.*, Series D 316, p. 141.
10.   *Ibid.*, Series H 599, p. 379.
11.   *Ibid.*, Series H 752, p. 385.
12.   *Ibid.*, Series D 725, p. 164.
13.   The poverty lines for 1905 and 1925 were $413 and $1,093, respectively. These were obtained from Oscar Ornati, *Poverty Amidst Affluence* (New York: Twentieth Century Fund, 1996), Table A, pp. 147-148. The average annual earnings for 1905 was $451 and for 1925 it was $1,253 (both in nominal dollars). These data were obtained from *Historical Statistics of the United States: Colonial Times to 1970*, Series D 723, p. 164.
14.   *Historical Statistics of the United States: Colonial Times to 1970*, Part 2, Series X 552, p. 1009.
15.   *Ibid.*, Series D 725, p. 164.
16.   The first estimate was made by Oscar Ornati, *Poverty Amidst Affluence* (New York: Twentieth Century Fund, 1996), and the second by Eugene Smolensky, "The Past and Present Poor," pp. 84-96 in Roger William Fogel and Stanley L. Engerman (eds.), *The Reinterpretation of American Economic History,* (New York: Harper and Row, Publishers, 1971).
17.   *Historical Statistics of the United States: Colonial Times to 1970*, Part 1, Series D 951, p. 178.
18.   *Ibid.*, Part 1, Series H 751, p. 385.
19.   Seymour L. Wolfbein, *Employment and Unemployment in the United States* (Chicago, IL: Science Research Associates, Inc., 1964), pp. 187-188. According to this author, this point was reached in 1957.
20.   C. Wright Mills, *White Collar* (New York: Oxford University Press, 1953).
21.   *Ibid.*, p. xvi.
22.   *Income, Poverty, and Health Insurance Coverage in the United States: 2006* (P60-233), U.S. Census Bureau, HHES Division (Washington, DC: USGPO, August 2007), Table B-1, p. 44.
23.   *Ibid.*, Table A-1, p. 29.
24.   Historical labor force statistics are available at the Bureau of Labor Statistics Web site, http://www.bls.gov.
25.   *Historical Statistics of the United States: Colonial Times to 1970:* Part 1, Series D 216 and Series D 217, p. 140.
26.   *Ibid.*, H 751, p. 385.
27.   Kevin M. Murphy and Finis Welch, "The Structure of Wages," *Quarterly Journal of Economics*, February 1992, pp. 215-326.
28.   Bureau of Labor Statistics, http://www.bls.gov.
29.   *Ibid.*
30.   *Ibid.*
31.   For a brief history of the events surrounding this new occupational classification, see the U.S. Census Bureau, *Statistical Abstract of the United States: 2003*, Washington, DC, 2003, p. 383.
32.   See U.S. Bureau of Labor Statistics, *BLS Releases 2000-2010 Employment Projections, News*, USDL 01-443, December 3, 2001.
33.   See the Bureau of Economic Analysis Web site at, http://www.bea.gov.
34.   *Ibid.*
35.   U.S. Census Bureau, http://www.census.gov.

36.   Dennis Gilbert, *The American Class Structure In An Age of Growing Inequality,* 5th Ed. (Belmont, CA: Wadsworth Publishing Company, 1998), p. 92.

37.   The family income data for 1929 and 1959 were adjusted for inflation and are charted in terms of 1962 dollars. They were obtained from Herman P. Miller, *Income Distribution in the United States: A 1960 Census Monograph,* (Washington, DC: USGPO, 1966), Table I-6, p. 14.

38.   Oscar Ornati, *Poverty Amidst Affluence* (New York: Twentieth Century Fund, 1996), Table A, pp. 147-148.

39.   See Herman P. Miller, *Income Distribution in the United States: A 1960 Census Monograph,* pp. 30-31 for a discussion of the poverty line during these years.

40.   According to the Bureau of Labor Statistics' Consumer Price Index for information and information processing (services and products), between 1995 and 2003, this price index fell from 98.9 to 87.8 (December, 1997 = 100.0). See U.S. Census Bureau, *Statistical Abstract of the United States: 2004-2005* (124th Edition), Washington, DC, 2004, no. 700, p. 465.

41.   *Ibid.,* no. 1150, p. 731.

42.   Thorstein Veblen, *The Theory of the Middle Class,* (New York: Random House, 1934), Ch. 4.

43.   C. Wright Mills, *White Collar* (New York: Oxford University Press, 1953), p. xvi.

44.   Robert Kuttner, "The Declining Middle," *The Atlantic,* July 1983, pp. 60-72.

45.   The Middle Class Misery Index, preumably, reflected changes in gas prices, incomes, tuitions, health costs, bankruptcies, home ownership, and jobs.

46.   Barbara Ehrenreich, *Fear of Falling* (New York: Pantheon Books, 1989).

6

Inside the Middle Class

The first lesson of modern sociology is that the individual cannot understand
his own experience or gauge his own fate without locating himself within the trends
of his epoch and the life chances of all the individuals of his social layer.
—C. Wright Mills

At the outset of this book (in the Preface and elsewhere) reference was made to the gloomy economic outlook that had overcome millions of Americans in late 2007 and early 2008. A future of declining house prices, growing home foreclosures, a weaker job market, higher food and fuel prices, sagging wages and incomes, and so on, all seemed to be drawing nearer.

Whether or not these events intensify and the economy enters a period of recession, and negative economic growth, only time will tell. Clearly, the nation's middle class has been through economic recessions before: for many persons, families, and households, belts were tightened, future plans were disrupted, adjustments to economic lifestyles were made. But in the end, and based on past experiences, the middle class has always survived—and flourished.

Regardless, of what happens in the future, it is a fact that the middle class in recent years has *already* been told that they are living in a sad state, economically. Indeed, from the mainstream media, news stories have reported how their jobs were being outsourced, their pensions were under funded, how they were having difficulties educating their kids, and how they were only living from paycheck to paycheck. In short, for many years they were told they were experiencing the "middle class squeeze"—and also who was to blame.

In a sense, this depiction of middle class life in the United States has contributed to the income gap muddle. Why—because not all of the middle class over recent decades had been affected by these problems to the extent reported by the media. Without question, parts of it have had economic difficulties, but certainly not all. Nevertheless, that was the message in the media's references to the "tough" economic conditions in the bottom 80 percent or 90 percent of this nation's income distribution.

In this chapter, our nation's middle class is divided into three component parts and analyzed in the context of certain problems confronting it—and the reality of the situation. The middle class, and its component parts, is defined entirely in terms of an annual household income definition as follows:

Lower middle class—$25,000 to $49,999
Middle middle class—$50,000 to $99,999
Upper middle class—$100,000 to $149,999

The use of such a definition for the middle class, of course, is open to dispute. In fact, any definition of the middle class can be debated considering the fact that even the Census Bureau—the nation's fact finder—has no definition.

Obviously, the above definition is simplistic and does not consider the many other factors that could be used in addition to income, such as education, residence, cultural pursuits, consumption patterns, etc. With respect to the purely income definition used above, it could be argued that the lower limit of the lower middle class ($25,000) is too low and the upper limit of the upper middle class ($149,999) is too high. Regarding the former, it is true that in 2006 some large families (five people or more) with an annual income of $25,000 would be classified as poor according to the poverty definition used by the Federal government.[1] But it is also true that given Americans' predilections for identifying themselves as members of the middle class, or at least working class, it is better to err on the side of C. Wright Mills' quote at the head of this chapter. Regarding the latter upper middle class limit, I would argue that it could legitimately be moved even higher given the frequency of families with two high earning couples as well as the incidence of assortative mating in today's society (i.e., men and women with similar socio-economic characteristics who marry). Having said all this about my definition, I can only say that typologies of any kind, the simple or complex, are prone to disagreement.

Clearly, with the above definition of the middle class in mind, this author believes that it has *neither* declined in size in recent decades *nor* is it struggling to the extent the mainstream media would have you believe. Rather, it has expanded and, for the most part, has prospered. It has expanded not only upward in the nation's income distribution but also downward (i.e., it morphed) because of the significant changes taking place in education, consumerism, and technology.

Traditionally, it has always been thought to be unfortunate if a family or a household had an annual income below average, or below the norm in society. But this is no longer true simply because the nation's average income has grown to such an extent in the last 100 years. In times past, to be below the average income was to be living in poverty or as the elite media like to call today, "working class."

It is also for another reason the working class moniker has been eschewed. In my opinion, the applicability of this title has eroded with the passage of time and the changing nature of society and its labor force. After all, most of us work (or have worked). Some work with computers and others with jack hammers, but we're all (most of us anyway) in the work force in one capacity or another. Working class was a term coined decades ago to contrast with another stratum of society, which was presumably better educated and employed in more skilled occupations. Indeed, today, based on average annual earnings alone, high school teachers would qualify for the lower middle class while elevator installers and repairmen would fall into the middle middle class.[2] Admittedly, the lower middle class is more akin to the working class of old and it confronts more economic problems than its counterparts above them, but working class as a descriptor is slowly becoming dated.

The upward expansion of the upper middle class, of course, is the stratum of society that the elite media fail to acknowledge and discuss to any extent. It is this upper middle class that is spearheading this nation's second middle class revolution. This is the stratum of society that has also contributed to the widening of the nation's income gap. Simply recall (from Figure 2.2) how the ratios of the 95th and 50th income percentiles grew over the last 39 years—from 2.70 ($98,012 relative to $36,847) in 1967 to 3.63 ($174,012 relative to $48,201) in 2006.[3]

No, America's middle class did not decline in the last 30 or 40 years. Indeed, it morphed, it spread out, and it has become more diverse than it ever has. And as has always happened, it suffered its bumps and bruises along the way, fed upon its self-doubts, but then moved onward—the backbone of the nation.

The Middle Class "Squeeze"

In response to the Census Bureau's release of the family income and poverty estimates for income year 2004, *The New York Times* wrote a harsh editorial entitled "Life in the Bottom 80 Percent."[4] It was directed at the then Congressional majority (Republicans), and, by extension, the Bush administration. Although the editorial was written three years ago, it does illustrate quite vividly how the "income gap" meaning has been changed by the media over a 40-year period—from economic problems of the poor to economic problems of the poor *and* the middle class.

According to the Census data for 2004, family incomes had not increased for a fifth straight year and the nation's poverty rate had moved up from 12.5 to 12.7 percent.[5] In response to these bad economic numbers, the *Times* wrote about the lack of income growth, the growing ranks of the poor, and the increase in the number of persons without health insurance—and then they concluded with the following: "Income inequality is an economic and social ill, but the administration and the Congressional majority don't seem to recognize that."

(You will recall from Chapter 1, how the *Times* more recently—in 2007—reported a story that everyone below the 99th percentile was not sharing in the nation's economic gains. So now, in just a few years, the income gap definition has been expanded upward to include everyone below the 99th percentile on one side of the gap—and the top percentile of the income distribution on the other.)

Household income at the 80th percentile of the nation's income distribution back in 2004 was $88,029—approximately 4.6 times greater than the official U.S. poverty threshold for a 4-person family in that year (two children under 18 years).[6] No doubt economic problems can exist for households at this income level (even above). But for a news outlet, of such high regard for many in this nation, to imply that economic life is bad for households at and below the 80th income percentile seemed an exaggeration.

It is from rhetoric like this that we not only have redefined the income gap to include the vast proportion of the nation's population on the bad side of the gap, but have brought into being a new phrase related to it, the middle class squeeze. This catchy terminology, of course, has become the mantra for some in the media and the political "left." If one doubts this, simply type in the middle class squeeze into any Internet search engine and count the "hits" from all sorts of groups, organizations, people, etc.

The squeeze on middle class families and households simply means too little *income* for the goods and services *needed* to live a middle class lifestyle. We have all heard about the rising cost of gasoline and other fuels, the cost of higher education, the cost of health insurance, the cost of future retirement, and on and on. And then, of course, we have also heard about stagnating incomes and wages, the outsourcing of jobs, and the sudden and unexpected layoffs.

For as much as one hears and reads about the squeeze on television, radio, in the newspapers, magazines, and on the Internet, just stop for a moment and ask yourself this question:

"Is $88,000 a year a trifling sum of money?"

Most likely, you'll reply: "It depends—it depends if I live in Manhattan, how many kids I have, what my health is, if I have a solid job, what my tastes are," and so on. In other words, "it depends" implies "conditions,"—things that are possible "if" such and such is a reality or fact.

As mentioned above, the "squeeze" supposedly comes about when *needs* are not completely satisfied because of inadequate *incomes*. The mainstream media has always assumed that the only way to ease up on the squeeze is by increasing incomes (or lowering prices) but never reducing needs. Why not? For a very simple reason: Can you imagine a presidential candidate campaigning around the country and addressing the middle class squeeze issue by advising the electorate to reduce their needs—to lower their expectations about buying that new car, or sending Johnny to a state university instead of an Ivy League school, or not going on that cruise to the Caribbean? No, needs and expectations have almost become synonymous in America and when they are not met, Americans become angry.

Robert J. Samuelson, a syndicated columnist, wrote two significant columns on this subject a few years back that are still quite relevant. In 2004 when the topic of the squeeze was red hot because of the presidential election he wrote that there was nothing new about the middle class squeeze because it's just part of who middle class Americans are. We simply expect to do better—it's this pressure inside all of us.[7] A couple of years later in late 2006 he wrote another revealing column based on some polling data about Americans and what they feel about the economy. Remember, this was at a time when the 2006 Congressional elections had already taken place and Iraq and the economy were the two main news stories of the day. Samuelson wrote that according to this particular poll, while 32 percent felt the economy wasn't performing too well, in terms of their own personal economic lives, 52 percent thought things were good to excellent. (You will recall, that before the election in 2006, the nation's unemployment rate was 4.7 percent and incomes and wages were on the rise.)

A number of solutions to the alleged middle class squeeze have been proposed in recent years (both by Democrats and Republicans because they realize the size of the middle class). In general, they involve economic interventions that are designed to impact family incomes or expenditures. For example, targeted middle class tax cuts were proposed a few years back by the Democrats in the 2004 presidential campaign, a prescription drug bill was passed into law a couple years ago during the Bush administration, and increasing the Federal minimum wage received considerable attention after the 2006 Congressional elections (more about this below). A couple of specific interventions are discussed below.

Economic Interventions

As everyone knows, one economic intervention was passed into law in 2007—a higher Federal minimum wage—as a result of the Congressional elections in 2006. It was increased from $5.15 an hour to $5.85 in the summer of 2007, and then to $6.55 by the summer of 2008, and then $7.25 by the summer of 2009. Many states in recent years have enacted their own minimum wage laws.

Another similar intervention has been the expansion of "living wage" ordinances.[8] A number of municipalities have adopted such ordinances. These laws require employees of employers who do business with a governmental authority to be paid at certain levels above the Federal government's poverty lines. Both have been popular mechanisms for raising wages by liberal politicians because, on the surface, they have such a humanitarian and common sense appeal.

Criticisms of raising the Federal minimum wage and expansion of living wage ordinances are similar. Empirical studies by economists have often provided conflicting results about the economic impact of raising the minimum wage and expanding living wage ordinances around the country, and adverse economic affects are possible. First, the cost of labor to employers is increased artificially creating possible disemployment affects. Unemployment among youths, immigrants, and other low-skilled, low productivity-type workers is likely to result. Furthermore, employers may decide to forgo hiring additional workers because of the increased labor cost, or worse, specific employers may decide to move their operations to other locales to avoid the increased labor costs.

Critics also say that such artificial means for enhancing family and household wages are poorly targeted. For example, in the case of the minimum wage, in 2006 about 51 percent of those workers receiving hourly wages at or below the Federal minimum were less than 25 years of age, in other words, young persons who were not strongly attached to the work force.[9] Furthermore, it appears that these low-wage workers have become a smaller and smaller proportion of all hourly paid workers—their proportion fell from about 13 percent in 1979 to just over 2 percent in 2006.[10]

Another more direct criticism of the concerns over low-wage workers is very simple: They *are* paid according to what they contribute. Low-wage workers receive low wages because their productivity is low, whether because of their lack of education, skill, or overall work performance. How many times have customers walked away from a fast food establishment or retail vendor of some kind because of the worker's lack of courtesy or indifference or inability to satisfy a customer's request? In my opinion, the issue of low-wage jobs is too often dropped at the feet of the employer and never at the feet of the employee. Doesn't an employee have a responsibility to his or her employer to justify what's in the paycheck?

The outsourcing of jobs has resonated with the American middle class, thanks in large part to the media and political left in this country who view it as a serious threat. In reality, its focal point on American industry has been particularly narrow—manufacturing and information technology jobs—and not very great. Nevertheless, the warning flags have been hoisted and the political clamor for somebody to do something, especially because it impacts the upper half of the income distribution, has reached a highly audible level.

Some interventionist-type solutions to outsourcing involve establishing protectionist trade policies. For example, legislation could be established to forbid governments (state and local) to deal with companies who have actively moved their operations out of the country. If a municipality's payroll or tax information is processed by a company that has engaged in outsourcing, the municipality would be obliged to cancel the contract, keeping this work activity for American workers, even though it would be cheaper to process the information in India, Russia, or some other low-wage country. Such an intervention would presumably save (or protect) the jobs of highly-trained and educated American workers.

Other approaches involve passing legislation or enacting ordinances setting an hourly wage, considerably above the Federal or state minimum and above the Federal poverty line. This wage would have to be paid to workers employed by businesses or companies that do work for the state or municipality. Employers, of course, who have managed to win state or municipal contracts, would have to pay workers the so-called "living wage" or else lose their contracts. Obviously, where ordinances have been adopted, wage scales are forced upward by the complying employers.

Fortunately, these solutions to this aspect of the middle class squeeze have not been acted upon extensively. One recent exception is the state of Maryland, which in 2007 passed a living wage bill which would require state contractors to pay their employees $11.30 an hour for work performed in the Washington-Baltimore corridor and $8.50 an hour in more rural parts of the state. Maryland would be first state to apply the law statewide.[11] Intervening into the operation of the local labor market may save some jobs but at the expense of raising labor costs for the local government and ultimately driving up taxes higher than they would have had to be. Consequently, an effort to help families and households from the middle class would, in the long run, eventually hurt them.

Perpetuating the "Squeeze" Myth

Like the income gap muddle, the middle class squeeze is perpetuated by the mainstream media and its reporting of the type of news and information that fits its agenda. An example of this occurred a few years ago by an organization that is frequently cited by two media elites, *The New York Times* and *The Washington Post*.

The Economic Policy Institute (EPI), a left-leaning think tank in Washington, DC, produced an analysis of the Census Bureau's income and poverty report for 2004.[12] It was accompanied by a graph, part of which is shown in Figure 6.1. The EPI chart showed the trend in real median household income between 2000 and 2004 as well as the trend in output per man-hour, or productivity. Rising productivity, or producing goods and services more efficiently, is an important element in creating greater profits for entrepreneurs and greater wages for workers.[13] The trend line for output per man-hour showed an increase of 14 percent while the line for real median household income depicted a slight decline of about 4 percent. The EPI, in contrasting these two trends, wanted to demonstrate that during the Bush Administration, workers (as represented by their household incomes) were not receiving their just return. EPI's claim was that the return was going to corporate America and therefore the economic recovery was unbalanced exacerbating income inequality.

If the EPI economists had replaced the household income trend with the trend in the real average hourly compensation of workers (from the Bureau of Labor Statistics), however, they would have shown that workers

Figure 6.1
Productivity, Income, and Compensation
2000 to 2004

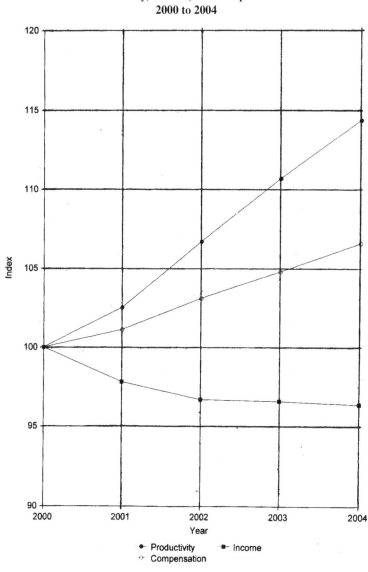

were indeed sharing in the benefits of increased labor productivity. This is also shown in Figure 6.1 by the trend line of real hourly compensation between 2000 and 2004—an upward trend of almost 7 percent over the period.

The reason the increase in hourly compensation did not translate into rising household income is primarily definitional. The household income statistics of the Census Bureau relate to money, or cash, income only from a variety of sources, not just employers. While the wages and salaries of workers would be included in Census Bureau income, that part of average hourly compensation composed of employers' contributions to workers' health insurance and other forms of "noncash" benefits provided workers would not be. This component of workers' compensation has grown rapidly in recent years.

The "Vulnerable" Lower Middle Class

It is to the lower middle class, or the underbelly of the middle class, that the elite media and liberal-oriented think tanks focus their attention and ask our government to pay more attention. According to them, the safety net is frayed and the underbelly is only a paycheck away from economic disaster. What are the facts?

The lower middle class, for this discussion, has been defined as any household whose annual income falls between $25,000 and $49,999. According to the Census Bureau, in 2006 there were 30.3 million households who had incomes in this range, or 26.1 percent of all households.[14]

As shown in Table 6.1 and based on Census Bureau data for 2002, households in the lower middle class are more likely to have householders who are older (65 and over), younger (less than 25), and more poorly educated than is the case of the middle middle class and upper middle class. In addition, the householder is much less likely to be a member of a married-couple family, and a full-time, year-round worker.

Because of these very basic characteristics, the lower middle class is less well prepared to support themselves through working in the labor market than members of the middle middle class and upper middle class. Furthermore, they are more dependent on income derived from sources other than the labor market, such as, retirement pension funds and government programs. In other words, households in the lower middle class are economically more vulnerable than are households in the higher income classes.

Let's further examine why this is the case. One principle reason for their vulnerability is the relatively low proportion of such households who are married couples. According to the Census data in Table 6.1, only 47 percent of the households in the lower middle class are composed of a husband and wife. What this means, of course, is that the other half of the households are devoid of, potentially, a second income provider, either from work in the labor market or previous work experience in the labor market (retirement income).

Table 6.1
Selected Characteristics (in percent) of Middle Class Income Groups, 2002

Characteristics	Lower Middle Class ($25,000 to $49,999)	Middle Middle Class ($50,000 to $99,999)	Upper Middle Class* ($100,000 to $149,999)
Percent	100.0	100.0	100.0
Age of Hhldr.:			
65 or over	20.5	9.7	7.1
Under 25	7.3	3.7	1.4
Type of Household:			
Family	67.3	81.0	87.7
Married couple	47.1	68.4	81.2
Female hhldr.	14.9	8.1	3.9
Nonfamily	32.7	19.0	12.3
Education of Hhldr:			
Less than H.S.	15.7	6.5	2.7
H.S. graduate	35.0	28.4	13.7
Bachelor degree or more	20.5	35.1	61.1
Work Experience of Hhldr.:			
Worked	72.4	87.6	90.4
Full-time, year around	52.1	68.7	74.8

Source: U.S. Census Bureau

* Characteristics for this income group include those households with annual incomes in 2002 of $150,000 or more. Of the 15.6 million households with incomes above $100,000 or more, 5.6 million had incomes of $150,000 or more.

Single-parenting, whether because of divorce, separation, adoption, or child-bearing out of wedlock, has been on the rise for many decades in the American culture. It is not without potential economic costs. In 2004, there were 14.0 million women householders and 4.9 million men householders—and approximately 40 percent of this total was from the lower middle class.[15] The difficulties of maintaining a family with children with only one income from a modestly paying job have been well documented both in the popular media and academic literature.

Another weakness in the economic armor of the lower middle class, of course, is its relatively low level of investment in human capital (i.e., education, skills, training). While 16 percent of householders in the $25,000 to $49,999 annual income range have less than a high school education, only 21 percent have a Bachelor's degree (i.e, college education) or more. This leaves a significant proportion (63 percent) of householders with only a high school diploma or a bit more of formal education—in a world of work, which today is increasingly demanding high skills and advanced training.

There are many ramifications for the lower middle class as a result of the marital and educational characteristics of these households. One of them concerns their ability to provide for their own health insurance coverage. In 2004, almost 1 out of every 3 persons without health insurance coverage for a full year was a member of a lower middle class family—or 14.8 million people.[16] The argument, of course, has been made that because of the relatively low annual incomes of lower middle class households and the high cost of health insurance, the United States has been negligent in not providing health insurance for these people from the lower middle class.

Obviously, when a primary bread winner of a household loses his or her job, the health insurance coverage often goes with it, since it is through employers that most Americans receive their health insurance coverage. That is a hard, cold reality. On the other hand, not all of these households lacking health insurance coverage are without householders holding jobs. Now, $25,000, or even $50,000, may not go far in providing food and clothing for a family and a roof over head, but neither are these inconsequential sums of money.

According to the Bureau of Labor Statistics' (BLS) Consumer Expenditure Survey in 2003, the average consumer unit (household) with an annual income of between $30,000 and $39,999 spent an average of $34,931 on various goods and services.[17] About 71 percent of that amount went for food, shelter, clothing, and transportation, leaving a total of $10,203 for other consumption items. (The expenditures are a little bit smaller below this income range and somewhat larger above.) Fully aware that the cost of providing health insurance coverage for a family is expensive (and always increasing), it would appear, nevertheless, that households in the lower middle class should be able to provide, at least, the most modest of health insurance coverage for their families. In the BLS survey just discussed, the average household in the $30,000 to $39,999 annual income range did spend $1,270 for health insurance.

The obvious question is, of course, what are the lower middle class households who do not have health insurance coverage spending their money on? The BLS survey shows that households in this income range have, on average, two vehicles and that 95 percent of the households own or lease one vehicle. Certainly many of them have the popular consumer durables that we see advertised in magazines, newspapers, and television as well as partake in the various consumer services (e.g., cell phone and Internet services) that our economy provides. Consequently, if health insurance is not available in many of these lower middle class households (containing 2.5 million children under 18 alone)—and it is considered in today's culture a virtual necessity—whose fault is it? What really is going on in many instances is not a middle class squeeze, but rather confusion over household priorities.

There is no doubt that the lower middle class probably contains many households that are in a state of economic transition and many in a state of economic vulnerability. Some are on their way up the income distribution, such as the just-married college graduates; others are on their way down either because of retirement or some economic calamity like a job loss or health problem. There is no doubt those households in this income class face more economic challenges and struggles to "make it in America." Nevertheless, I would submit that these households should be considered in the middle class—and probably most of them do as well.

The "Viable" Middle Middle Class

Moving up the Nation's income ladder a couple rungs one arrives at the heart of the nation's middle class where 34.2 million households had annual incomes of between $50,000 and $99,999 in 2006. Some would disagree that this is the middle because in 2006, the median income, or mid-point of the income distribution was $48,201. However, it is also important to point out that the mean, or average household income in that year was $66,570.[18]

Recall now that according to *The New York Times* in August of 2005, economic life was supposedly "pretty darn tough" for most of the households in this part of the distribution (or at least those between $50,000 and $88,000 a year). According to this newspaper, the middle class squeeze was no doubt very much in evidence for households in this income range. So, let's investigate the middle middle class.

Again, there is no doubt that some families feel (and have felt) economic pressure—but who hasn't and when—when you are calling yourself "middle class?" This is what happens in this part of the income distribution from time-to-time in a free market, capitalistic country like the United States.

As was implied in the discussion of the lower middle class, economic life in the middle middle class is less perilous, somewhat more secure, indeed, one might even call it "viable." Certainly clouds sometimes do appear on the horizon—as they are in late 2007 and early 2008—for many of these households, but by and large, the future should be bright. Why?

Table 6.1 displays an abundance of positive characteristics that makes their life in a market economy "do-able." First, households in the middle middle class are mostly composed of married couples (68 percent); second, the vast majority of them have a householder in the prime working years of 25 to 64 (86 percent); third, a significant proportion of the households hold a Bachelor's degree or more (35 percent); and fourth, the vast majority of the householders work full time the year around (69 percent).

Two issues of the middle class squeeze that have had enormous importance for middle middle class households (according to the elite media) concern the role of the working wife and the cost of educating their children. Everyone knows that the role of the working wife has become a topical issue in modern day America. One aspect of the debate about working wives that has been heard in a variety of circles is quite basic: Is it an economic necessity or not that the wife work? Typically, left-leaning organizations, think tanks, and social commentators argue emphatically that it is an economic necessity because the wages and salaries paid to their husbands have not kept up with the cost of living. Similar groups, but of a more conservative persuasion, suggest it is a more open matter and that one has to consider the changing role of women in modern society. Both sides would agree, however, that with the rise of feminism, the role of women in society has indeed changed, whether one considers education, entertainment, the military, or whatever cultural domain.

But one fact is obvious. If living the American Dream means accumulating wealth and attaining the highest standard of living that can possibly be obtained, in the current day and age, one's chances are best in a husband-wife family—and especially if both partners are in the paid labor force. The median household earnings of a husband in a married couple family in which the wife worked as well in 2004 was $77,312, and the wife's median earnings was $25,861—and these were *medians* meaning half of the husbands and half of the wives earned even more.[19]

It is very easy to observe this positive impact of working wives on family incomes across the income distribution. Figure 6.2 shows the proportion of working wives in married couple households across in-

Figure 6.2
Working Wives by Household Income
(as a percent of all households, 2004)

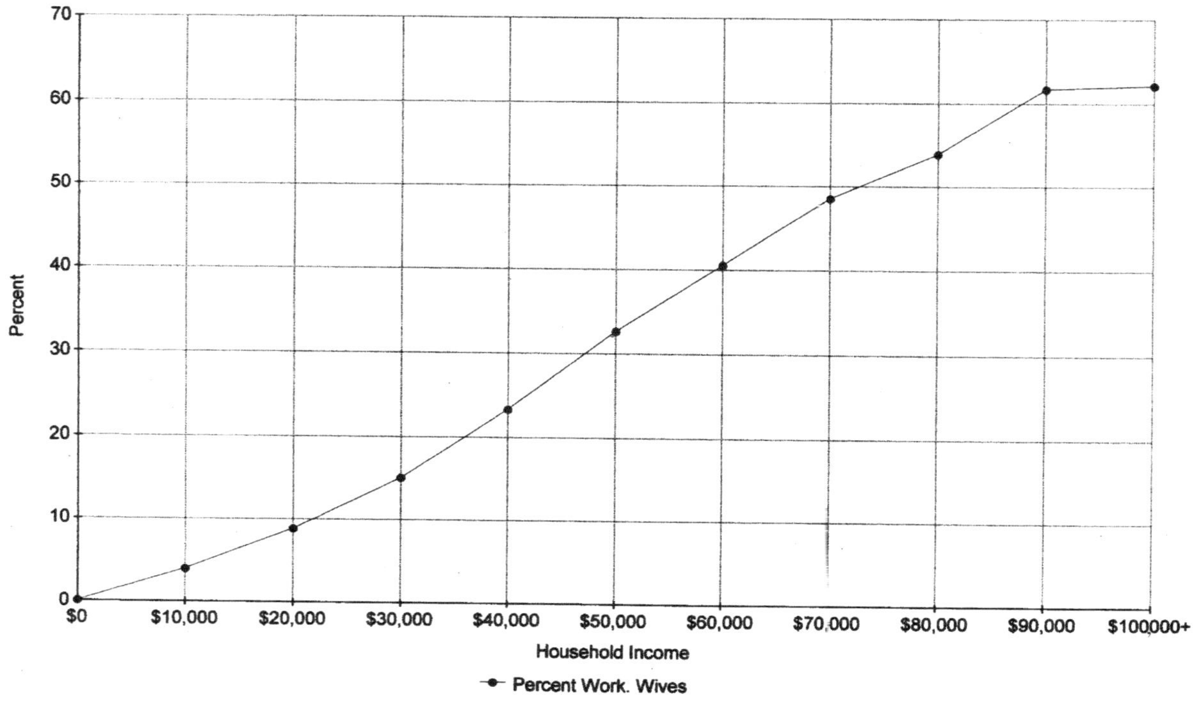

Percent

Household Income

→ Percent Work. Wives

come classes—from the income classes in the lower class on upward to those over the $100,000 level. As one marches up the income distribution, the proportion of households with a working wife rises slowly, but consistently. For example, the incidence of working wives in 2004 in lower middle class households rose from 12 percent to 32 percent, but in the middle middle class households it increased from 33 percent to 62 percent or so, and then moves onto even higher levels.

Two factors account for this growth in the proportion, one purely statistical and the other cultural. As discussed above, the lower middle class is made up of about one-half married-couple families and the other half of households of other types of families and households—so at best, only about one-half of all lower middle class households could have a working wife in them. It would be a statistical impossibility for them to have more. But as the proportion of married-couple families rises as we move up the income distribution, the possibility of these households having working wives in them rises as well.

The second reason for the growth in the proportion of households with working wives is cultural—the social acceptability of wives to work in the labor market. The long-term trend in the rise of women's labor force participation, which began during WWII, has been well documented. What has not been documented or understood, however, was the profound affect of this trend on the nation's *second* middle class revolution. The widening of the income gap, as we read and hear about it today, is very much related to this successful entry of women into the labor force. Women entered the work force because the economic returns to do so where greater than the returns for staying at home. Not only that, but growing evidence has indicated an additional trend toward "positive assortative mating," that is, men and women with similar socio-economic characteristics becoming married. Growing proportions of well-educated men have been marrying well-educated women—and both have been working in high-paying jobs. But the fuller story of this development is discussed in the following section. Suffice it to say that the assistance of a wife's paycheck has undoubtedly contributed to the viability of the millions of middle middle class households.

Another aspect of the middle class squeeze concerns the difficulty middle class households have in providing college educations for their children. As we have been told, tuitions, room and board, text books, and all the other costs associated with college educations have soared in recent decades.[20] Some media observers have therefore concluded that it is virtually impossible for the children of middle class families to go to college. The resulting impact on the middle middle class was as expected.

Since it is from the middle class, especially its middle middle, that millions of prospective college students come, a closer look at this aspect of the middle class squeeze is provided. The U.S. Department of Education's National Center for Education Statistics publishes information on college costs.[21] Indeed, in their calculation of the "average net price of college" they factor in tuition and other expenses, such as the cost of living of a dependent, undergraduate student, under age 24, but minus all grants and loans that are received. Their estimate of the annual cost of a college education at a public 4-year institution in 1989-1990 was $8,900 and in 1999-2000 it was $10,500, an increase of 18 percent in constant 1999 dollars. At a private, not for profit institution, the comparable figures were $15,500 and $17,700, for an increase of 14 percent.

While these are formidable increases in college costs, it would appear that a married couple in which both the husband and wife worked could handle them. The Bureau of the Census reported that between the year 1990 and the year 2000, the median annual income of a married couple in which the wife worked rose from $62,409 to $72,299 (in constant 2002 dollars), an increase of almost 16 percent.[22] Obviously, if Mom and Dad were putting two or three college-age children through school at the same time, the budget would be tight. Nevertheless, it could be done, with much thanks to the working wife. Did she work because she had to, or because she wanted to? Unfortunately, the answers are still hidden in the statistics.

The "Victorious" Upper Middle Class

It may be presumptuous to describe a segment of the middle class as victorious. But indeed, if someone doesn't, it is certain the mainstream media will not. They are victorious in the sense that they have pushed the boundary of the middle class upwards to regions never before thought possible—and they live (most of them) a dream that is the envy of the rest of the world's citizens: the American Dream. Sure, they can experience their economic calamities too (like their neighboring cohorts below), but their chances of recovery, I would argue, are pretty high as well.

The upper middle class in 2006, as defined here, consists of households with annual incomes of between $100,000 and $149,999—sums of money that their mothers and fathers and needless to say their grandparents would find impossible only a couple of decades ago. Although this component of the middle class is not as large as the middle middle and lower middle, it is of significant size—and, more importantly, growing (even during economic downturns)!

In 2006, the number of households in this income category totaled 13.4 million, or 11.5 percent of all households in the nation, a somewhat smaller representation than the middle middle and lower middle classes.[23] Households with incomes above this level, say up to $200,000, have many of the same socio-economic characteristics and, it could be argued that they too should be considered upper middle class—indeed, they could be called the "upper middle class-plus." They numbered 4.8 million households in 2006. And beyond the $200,000 mark, there exists another 4.0 million households around the country—and here we can really begin speaking of the upper class, or rich.

To gain some perspective on the remarkable increase over the years in households with incomes between $100,000 and $149,999, we can consult the Census Bureau's statistics on real household incomes by income class between 1976 and 2006.[24] The number of households with real annual incomes of $100,000 or more rose from 5.1 million (or 6.9 percent of the total) to 22.1 million (or 19.1 percent). Now, not all of these households are of the Warren Buffet, Bill Gates, and Donald Trump type, although they too would be included here. But as was shown above, in 2006 the upper middle class numbered 13.4 million, a *very* significant part of all households with incomes over $100,000. And if we added in the households with income between $150,000 and $199,999—those in the upper middle class-plus—the upper middle class would total 18.1 million of the total 22.1 million households with incomes above $100,000. So, to say the least, the upper middle class has mushroomed in 30 years.

The upper middle class, relative to the middle middle and lower middle class, is the best educated, most married, and the most strongly attached to the labor force (see Table 6.1 for selected characteristics of households with annual incomes above $100,000).[25] Indeed, their success in the world of work can be sensed by examining the occupational distribution of men and women with annual earnings just below, as well as, above the $100,000 level in 2004, shown in Table 6.2

Of the 6.4 million men and the 1.4 million women in 2004 with annual earnings above $100,000, approximately 3 out of every 4 worked in management, professional, and related occupations.[26] Both the men and women in this group of occupations had similar concentrations in jobs as managers in business and financial operations—about 40 percent. With respect to their roles in professional occupations, both had significant representations in jobs associated with the health, legal, and computer

Table 6.2
Occupation Distribution of Men and Women with
Annual Earnings of $95,000 to $99,999 and $100,000 or More, 2004

Occupation	$95,000 to $99,999		$100,000 or more	
	Men	Women	Men	Women
Percent	100.0	100.0	100.0	100.0
Managerial and Professional Specialty	71.5	83.4	72.2	77.7
Management, business, and financial	36.7	49.1	40.0	41.7
Professional and related	34.8	34.3	32.2	36.1
Computer, mathematical	11.1	5.9	5.1	4.1
Architecture, engineering	11.7	-	4.9	0.6
Legal	2.5	-	6.2	6.4
Health practitioner and technical	4.0	13.0	10.1	15.7
Service	3.5	-	2.0	2.2
Sales and Office	11.7	14.8	17.0	18.4
Natural Resources, Construction, Maintenance	7.2	-	3.4	-
Production, Transportation, Material Moving	6.0	-	4.9	1.5
Armed Forces	0.3	-	-	-

Source: U.S. Census Bureau

fields (e.g., doctors, lawyers, computer scientists), while the men were also quite prevalent in engineering and architectural domains. It is interesting to note also that the three quarters of a million men and women with annual earnings in the $95,000-$99,999 range—the "cusp" of the upper middle class—had an occupational profile that was very similar.

One of the primary reasons (besides educational attainment and high paying jobs) that many households in the last quarter century or so have made it into the upper middle class is the "dual earner" phenomenon alluded to in the previous section. The upper middle class is the "homeland" of the married couple family—where the vast majority of the households are composed of a husband, wife, and most likely, children. And the working wife has been, in many instances, the difference between a middle middle class lifestyle and an upper middle class lifestyle.

Figure 6.2 displays the proportion of households with wives in the paid labor force across the household income distribution in 2004. As was shown earlier, the incidence of working wives rises as household income rises. At the "cusp" of the upper middle class the proportion is above 60 percent—and for all households over an annual income of $100,000 it is also above 60 percent. Although the Census Bureau does not publish the statistics necessary to examine the phenomenon above the lower boundary of the upper middle class ($100,000), it no doubt continues upward and eventually levels off at annual incomes above the upper boundary of the upper middle class ($149,999) or beyond.

Dual earner families have been the subject of much research in recent years. While much of it concerns the ramifications of the decision of the wife to leave the home and seek employment, the fact is that wives have entered the work force largely in response to women's rising labor market opportunities, rather than due to declining opportunities of their husbands.[27] Indeed, this makes sense when one considers the changes that have taken place in women's educational opportunities over the last 50 years. As a consequence, similarly educated men and women marry and form households—and both go to work. In many instances, the role of the husband as the primary breadwinner for the household now becomes merged with the wife's role as an additional breadwinner because her earnings may be equal to or greater than her husband's.[28]

Evidence exists that dual earner families have played an important role in the widening income gap, along with shifts in the composition of households (i.e., from married-couple households to single-parent and nonfamily households).[29] This is because the earnings of women, who for many years earned only a small fraction of men's earnings, have begun to catch up to those of men, thereby diminishing the once-upon-a-time equalizing affect of women's earnings on family incomes (i.e., when women with low earning husbands entered the work place, they tended to "equalize" the family income distribution because their earnings along with their husbands pulled them closer to the families with high earning husbands). The growing tendency for well-educated and well-paid women to marry well-educated and well-paid men, or positive assortative mating, and its role in the nation's income gap, is one of the least discussed phenomenons in today's elite media.

It is certainly not the case that by simply having the wife join the husband in the work force assures economic success, or an annual income in excess of $100,000. Costs are incurred: child care, added transportation costs (i.e., gasoline, cars, bus and subway fares), clothing, and grooming costs. Every now and then we read or hear in the media how a family with dual earners and an income in the six figures is "struggling" to get by. But struggling is a relative term and not conducive to interpersonal comparisons. The fact remains: a married couple that is well-educated and trained for employment in today's work force is more likely to be in the upper middle class than a lesser endowed couple, single parent, or single individual—simply because they have a better opportunity to "make it" in the world of work.

In Summary

The middle class at the opening of the twenty-first century is considerably larger and more heterogeneous than the middle class at the halfway point of the twentieth century. Because it covers a much wider range of the income distribution than ever before, it's susceptibility to the economic ups and downs of a free market, capitalistic system has become more pronounced—but as the exposure to economic risk has become greater so has the exposure to economic opportunity.

The second middle class revolution is all about economic opportunity and those who have availed themselves of it. There is nothing to fear about an income gap that has been created as a result of economic opportunity—nor is there anything unfair about it.

Notes

1. *Income, Poverty, and Health Insurance Coverage in the United States* (P60-233), U.S. Bureau of the Census, HHES Division (Washington, DC: USGPO, August 2007), p. 43.
2. U.S. Bureau of Labor Statistics, National Occupational Employment and Wage Estimates, May 2004, *http://www.bls.gov*.
3. This ratio, of course, incorporates the expansion of the middle middle class as well.
4. *The New York Times,* "Life in the Bottom 80 Percent," Sept. 1, 2005, p. A22.
5. *Income, Poverty, and Health Insurance Coverage in the United States* (P60-229), U.S. Bureau of the Census, HHES Division (Washington, DC: USGPO, August 2005), p. 3 and p. 9.
6. That threshold was $19,157 in 2004. See, *Income, Poverty, and Health Insurance Coverage in the United States* (P60-229), p. 45.
7. Robert J. Samuelson, "Pressure of the American Dream," *The Washington Post,* July 26, 2004, p. A11, and "Myths and the Middle Class," *The Washington Post,* Dec. 27, 2006, p. A19.
8. Living wage ordinances are found typically in local governments where, by law, private companies who contract with the government for various goods and services are required to pay their employees a wage at some level above Federal poverty thresholds (e.g., 125 percent, 150 percent).
9. U.S. Bureau of Labor Statistics Internet web site, Characteristics of Minimum Wage Workers: 2006, *http://www.bls.gov*.
10. *Ibid.*

11. John Wagner and Lisa Rein, "Md. Bans Smoking, Approves Wage Bill," *The Washington Post,* April 10, 2007, pp. A1, A4.
12. Economic Policy Institute, "Income Picture," *http://www.epinet.org.*
13. Norman Frumkin, *Tracking America's Economy,* 3rd ed. (Armonk, NY: M.E. Sharpe & Co., 1998), p. 222.
14. *Income, Poverty, and Health Insurance Coverage in the United States: 2006* (P60-233), U.S. Bureau of the Census, HHES Division (Washington, DC: USGPO, August 2007), Table A-1, p. 29.
15. *Income, Poverty, and Health Insurance Coverage in the United States: 2004* (P60-229), p. 4, and Census Bureau Web site at, *http://www.census.gov.*
16. *Ibid.,* p. 7.
17. U.S. Bureau of Labor Statistics, Consumer Expenditure Survey, 2003, *http://www.bls.gov.*
18. *Income, Poverty, and Health Insurance Coverage in the United States: 2006,* (P60-233), Table A-1, p. 29. The reason the mean is higher than the median is that the value of the former is influenced more than the latter by higher incomes in the distribution.
19. U.S. Census Bureau Web site at, *http://www.census.gov.*
20. According to the Bureau of Labor Statistics' Consumer Price Index for All Urban Consumers (1982-84 = 100.0) the price index for college tuition and fees rose from 266.3 in August 1995 to 480.4 in August 2005, or by 80.4 percent.
21. See, U.S. Department of Education, National Center for Education Statistics, "The Condition of Education, 2004," Table 5, p. 19.
22. U.S. Census Bureau, *Statistical Abstract of the United States: 2004-2005,* No. 674, p. 448.
23. U.S. Census Bureau Web site at, *http://www.census.gov.*
24. *Income, Poverty, and Health Insurance Coverage in the United States: 2006* (P60-233), Table A-1, p. 29.
25. Unfortunately, the Census Bureau does not publish statistics in its annual income reports reflecting the characteristics of households in specific income ranges above the $100,000 level (e.g., $100,000 to $149,999).
26. U.S. Census Bureau Web site at, *http://www.census.gov.* Because this discussion is based on all persons in occupations with annual earnings above $100,000, it includes, by definition, the occupations of those persons with annual earnings above the upper middle class boundary of $149,999 and, therefore, is not exactly representative of the upper middle class occupational profile.
27. Chinhui Juhn and Kevin Murphy, "Wage Inequality and Family Labor Supply," *Journal of Labor Economics,* 15, No. 1, Part 1, (January 1997), pp. 72-97.
28. See Anne E. Winkler, "Earnings of Husbands and Wives in Dual-Earner Families," *The Monthly Labor Review,* April, 1998, pp. 42-48.
29. Lynn A. Karoly and Gary Burtless, "Demographic Change, Rising Earnings Inequality, and the Distribution of Personal Well-Being, 1959-1989," *Demography,* August, 1995, pp. 379-405.

7

So, Forget about the CEOs and the Top 1 Percent!

There is an inverse relationship between reliance on the state and self-reliance.
William F. Buckley, Jr.

Critics of the free market, capitalistic system must remember one thing about America: Wealth happens! And it happens not only for the likes of Bill Gates, Warren Buffett, and the others in the top 1 percent of the income distribution, it happens, albeit in smaller amounts, for the little guys in this country. It happens because, among the many goals of the American Dream, which have evolved over time, becoming rich is still one of them. Indeed, only in recent decades has the *corpus Americana* awakened once again to the fact that there is nothing wrong with wanting to be rich—and even richer.

Forgetting Our Fears

One of the most unfortunate notions that has worked itself into the body politic in recent years is that striving for wealth is bad for society. But this always happens when people become *too* economically successful. It happened when the country moved from the nineteenth into the twentieth century, and alas, it has happened once again.

Plutocracy, this is what is supposed to be our chief worry. As my dictionary defines it, that means: 1) government by the wealthy; and 2) a wealthy class that controls the government.[1] From this, supposedly, all the evil things we read about in the papers and hear about on television concerning the nation's income gap spread.

One of the principal proponents of the plutocracy thesis is Kevin Phillips, the political and economic commentator. In his interesting book, *Wealth and Democracy*, he spells out the similarities between the Gilded Age of the late nineteenth and early twentieth centuries and the past years of the late twentieth and early twenty-first centuries.[2] In his opinion, during both periods our society was drifting towards plutocracy. And with respect to today, his closing lines of the book are, to say the least, ominous:

> As the twenty-first century gets underway, the imbalance of wealth and democracy in the United States is unsustainable, at least by traditional yardsticks. Market theology and unelected leadership have been displacing politics and elections. Either democracy must be renewed, with politics brought back to life, or wealth is likely to cement a new and less democratic regime—plutocracy by some other name.[3]

A vision of the nineteenth century's "robber barons" comes quickly to mind—seated around a banquet table at a swanky hotel in Washington DC, chortling and smoking cigars.

Those suggesting that plutocracy is just around the corner are very serious. They sell books and give speeches and their material often ends up in left-leaning organizations, in short, spreading the message about the nation's wealthiest. In my opinion, they are saying that the wealthy are jeopardizing the nation's future by their greed, arrogance, privilege, and extravagant lifestyles.

After more than two centuries, this nation's legal system has been able to deal with the corporate scandals and abuses, just as was done 100 years ago. The officials of Enron, Tyco, WorldCom, Adelphia, and other corporations have been or are in the process of being dealt with just as the heads of Standard Oil, the Northern Pacific Railway, and the Northern Securities Company were called before authorities.[4]

Yes, sometimes bad things happen on the way to building an economy and creating economic growth. Sometimes in this process the life savings of people are lost, their jobs are taken away from them, and their futures are destroyed. Sometimes the reputations of whole industries are brought into question, like the savings and loan industry several years ago and the uranium mining industry many years ago. There is no question that the market machinery of capitalism can run rough and wild at times.

But, it also produces great wealth for society.

Take away the Vanderbilts, the Edisons, the Rockefellers, the Carnegies, the Harrimans, the Flaglers, and the other captains of American industry in the late nineteenth and early twentieth century and would the seeds ever have been planted for the first middle class revolution? Take away the Gates, the Dells, the Bezos, and the Waltons and the other business giants of the late twentieth and early twenty-first century and would we have seen the beginnings of the second middle class revolution?

Where would this nation be if over the years gone by we wiped away the top 1 percent of the wealth holders in this country? The answer is simple: We would be a "back-in-the-pack" country. Can one seriously think that without the rich of this nation that our gross domestic product would be the highest in the world? Are we really so sure that, on balance, it would have been better that we *not* had the "old" Gilded Age and today's "new" Gilded Age (as it has been called), even though both had their excesses?

Celebrating Economic Success

As a Census Bureau economist involved with studying the nation's income distribution some years ago, I was sometimes asked to brief government officials about what was happening to income inequality. On one such occasion back in the early 1990s, I was called upon to brief a member of Congress "on the hill." Two other economists were invited to the briefing as well.

The meeting took place in the Congressperson's office on a cold, winter's evening around 6 PM. Besides being nervous about the whole affair, I was also irritated because at that hour I was supposed to be on my way home. After a 10 or 15 minute wait for the Congressperson to appear in the office, the door swung open and the smiling legislator strode in, a hand extended in the direction of the three somewhat fearful economists, a well-dressed staff trailing.

I shall never forget one incident that occurred during the briefing. The Congressperson was seated next to me and we were all showing tables and charts containing income distribution data. One statistical table in particular caught the legislator's eye because it showed the top end of the income distribution (i.e., those households with annual incomes of $100,000 or more). While pointing downward at the top end of the distribution this representative of the people said, "Aha, so these are the ones!" It struck me as if Inspector Clouseau (of Peter Sellers' fame) had just found the culprit.

After thinking about this incident for some time, I felt the remark was an unfortunate expression of disdain for the economically successful of this nation. Perhaps it wasn't meant that way, but that was how it came across. (We touched upon class bias towards the rich in Chapter 3—and how it has come to permeate, once again, a significant part of our society.) But the Congressperson's performance that night brought home to me another, unfortunately sad, aspect of the income gap muddle: Why don't we celebrate economic success in this country?

No doubt, beneath the Congressperson's finger there were many rich people who had inherited their fortunes or earned them unfairly, and many CEOs who are now in jail or on their way. But it's almost certain there are many, many more who invested wisely and built their companies and businesses to become economic behemoths. What about some of the names that pop up in the media today, like Bill Gates, Michael Dell, or Warren Buffett, or some of those old tycoons from yesteryear, like Henry Ford, Andrew Carnegie, or Marshall Field?

And even further down beneath the finger one could find the millions of rich people who carried out the orders and plans of these economic titans—the chief financial officers, the vice-presidents, the senior executives sitting on mahogany row. Hasn't it been through their planning, efforts, and decisions, that millions of other Americans had jobs and could strive for a better life?

A Salute to Builders of "Big" Wealth

We don't celebrate the rich, I suppose, because they have everything and we don't—or at least considerably less than what they have. It's sort of like the old Hemingway quotation about why the rich are different from the rest of us: "Yes, they have more money." So why bother to celebrate them if that's the only difference.

But there's more to it than just that. For one thing, it's a matter of *how* they got rich. If it was through illegal or unfair machinations then we certainly wouldn't want to celebrate their economic success. For example, Bernie Ebbers, the former CEO of WorldCom and multimillionaire, did some things illegally and a jury found him guilty. He certainly didn't help the cause of reducing class bias directed at the rich. Then there is the matter of inherited wealth—"old money" as it is sometimes called. I think Americans tolerate these rich people as long as they don't "screw up" somehow, like those who simply flit away family fortunes.

A more subtle reason for why we don't celebrate the rich, however, might involve the marketplace. For the many rich people in this country who earned their fortunes on the up-and-up, some of us may be harboring envy deep down. Not envy for their goods and possessions necessarily, but rather something else—simply their success in the marketplace. They've succeeded to a much greater degree than we did, for whatever the reason—maybe they were smarter, shrewder, more willing to take a chance, maybe just lucky. And because they beat us, we feel some resentment towards them—as if they really didn't deserve to be living in that twenty-one-room mansion or sailing that seventy-five-foot yacht.

Of course, if they beat us fairly at this game of free market capitalism, then we shouldn't have anything to complain about. This is what America is all about—at least for most Americans. Maybe it is not necessarily making a million dollars by the time one is twenty-five years of age or having three houses and a fleet of cars, but having money is important for the vast majority of us—having *enough* money. But one person's enough is not another person's enough. The point is that the goal for most of us in this free market, capitalist society is acquiring *our* "enough."

If, indeed, that is the goal of our society than we shouldn't really harbor any resentment that someone beats us in this game of acquisition. Moreover, if we were truly good citizens, we should be happy for the guy or gal (guys or gals) that beat us at the game. Isn't that the American way? We aren't supposed to be sore losers, or that's what my parents taught me. If I got beat, I got beat—go on home and lick your wounds, but first, congratulate your opponent.

So why don't we celebrate the success of Bill Gates, Warren Buffett, and the Waltons, and all the others who made their fortunes on the up-and-up? The truth is that many of us really do celebrate their wealth in our quiet ways; we do applaud their success in making their fortunes because we know that in doing so they've also helped us. Not directly, not by showering us with twenty-dollar bills as they drive by in their limousines but by providing us with economic benefits, like jobs, products, low prices, and so forth. This is something the majority of Americans truly understand.

No, the ones who don't celebrate the success of our country's billionaires, millionaires, and those in the upper class called rich—but rather point to them and cry "foul"—are the "anointed anti-capitalists" in our midst.[5] They are the thinkers and dogmatists for the demonstrators racing through the streets when the finance ministers of the world's nations come to the World Bank in Washington, DC or for the protesters shutting down city blocks when Presidents of the G-7 nations meet in Genoa. They are the ones who teach their troopers to hate the capitalists' words, like profit, self-interest, markets, oil, and dollars. These avuncular elitists provide the rhetoric for the empty-headed youths who would have a much more hopeful future if they were behind their school desks reading Adam Smith rather than scrawling their inflammatory messages on the granite walls of banks.

What drives the anointed anti-capitalists to the edge of the cliff is the conjunction of the free market with a democratic form of government such as it exists today in the United States. For them the result of such a union is a society slowly being shredded—to be left with only a mushrooming poverty class, a withering middle class, and a handful of "plutocrats." But it is this sacred conjunction that has been the blessing of the United States, the wealthiest nation the world has ever seen. It is just this conjunction that has been the fertile breeding ground for the individuals who built their fortunes because they had the imagination and courage to see the economic possibilities of this nation.

It is this entrepreneurial and acquisitive drive embodied in the human spirit of those wealth-builders of today and of yesteryear that must be celebrated and applauded. Not to do so is a sacrilege and denies the basic meaning of America; not to do so is social suicide.

Cheers for the Upper Middle Class

Every year, after the Census Bureau releases the nation's income and poverty statistics for the previous calendar year, our office would be swamped with telephone calls and inquiries from the media. They wanted more information, more insight into what the statistics meant. I remember back in the early 1990s, a reporter from one of the nation's major newspapers asked me, "Who were the winners and losers last year?"

I wasn't naïve. For a civil servant in a nonpolitical job, this was a dangerous question. But it was a question that seemed to be in vogue those days, because the country had just come through a recession, Bill Clinton had just been elected President, and the news of the growing income gap was in the air. Depending on my answer, I could easily find myself in the pages of this "elite" newspaper the next morning—and, most likely, in hot water.

The question bothered me then, as it bothers me now. Here's a "hot-shot" reporter hoping to get this government economist to say something like, "Well, the incomes of the rich, or the highest fifth of the income distribution went up last year, while those for lowest fifth didn't change much at all," because that's indeed what happened.[6] He wanted me to say this because it would show, at least implicitly, the "victim and culprit" characters that would highlight his news story the next day concerning how this nation's economic system was so unfair and unjust.

What I truly wanted to say was this: "Yes, those at the top of the income distribution, especially the top 1 percent, did very well, indeed, they led us out of the recession like they usually do!" That would have been a true statement also, but, of course, I didn't say that. I liked my job too much. What I do recall saying was something like this: "The median annual household income between 1992 and 1993 declined slightly...I'm not sure I know what you mean by winners and losers." This ended the conversation and, needless to say, my name did not appear in the newspaper the next day.

The point of this little recollection should be obvious. This reporter didn't want to "celebrate" the good economic news for the top fifth of the income distribution; he only wanted to report how unfair our economic system was.

As was indicated in the previous chapter, the "victorious" upper middle are well educated and trained, employed primarily in managerial and professional jobs, and for the most part, are members of married-couple families—in other words, they've done all the right things for success in the new economy of the twenty-first century. They should be congratulated. But was it luck or did they know something that the less economically successful didn't know?

I would argue that it was the latter. Thanks in large measure to the entrepreneurs and investors who provided the "seed" money for much of the information technology industry and its related industries, the beneficiaries of their investment were the upper middle class. These are the members of our economy's new division of labor who are capable of "expert thinking" and "complex communication."[7] Like two hands coming together, the technology and the human capital meshed as if they were meant for each other.

The similarity of these recent events, which some have referred to as our information age revolution, with events from years past, like the period of industrialization in the first half of the twentieth century, are startling. In both periods, there was an upsurge of technological innovations (electricity, automobiles, radio, for example, in the first, and computers, telecommunication, television, for example, in the second) and a capable supply of labor to exploit them (a steadily growing and increasingly educated working class in the first and a highly educated and skilled middle class in the second). Both periods resulted in middle class revolutions, and behind each lay cultural and attitudinal changes about life in America—which ignited them.

For an ignition to occur, just as in lighting a fire, conditions must be just right, otherwise there will be no ignition. In the first half of the twentieth century, what were these conditions? In the very early years of that century, what changed on the part of society was a new attitude about the "hope and promise" of America. It was an attitude that was brought into the nation by the hordes of immigrants who arrived from Europe looking for a better life. They, more than many others today in contemporary society, understood well the rules of the game and how it was played. The only way to make the American Dream come true was to work for it.

Hope and promise have always been in evidence in the land. Indeed, its legacy can be traced back to the revolution. But like all human phenomenon, it ebbs and flows like the water in a tidal marsh. During the great immigration of those early years of the last century, the tidal flow of hope and promise reached staggering heights. And fortunately, the captains of industry had prepared the path for them with economic opportunities.

Fast forward to the late twentieth and early twenty-first centuries and one sees cultural and attitudinal changes occurring much like the hopeful patches of blue sky appearing on a cloud-filled day. Again the signs of "hope and promise" appear, this time not only by new inflows of immigrants but also by the sons and daughters of the middle class that had emerged earlier in the century. It was the hope and promise to create an even better life than what their parents had and what they grew up with—it was to reach even higher.

But the signs of hope and promise are often blown about by the "anointed anti-capitalists" who would rather level the playing field and provide a "guarantee" of a successful economic life for everyone. The upper middle has been told that there is more to life than just work and money; that their hopes and promises are simply based on cheap materialism; that they must stop and smell the flowers. Fortunately, they keep hopes and promises in front of them because they realize that there is nothing wrong in wanting to be rich, or, in less inflammatory language, in wanting to have enough!

So, it is to these members of the upper middle class who have awakened to the hope and promise of the nation's economy and the opportunities it provides everyone that a hearty cheer is offered.

For All the Other Economically Successful—Job Well Done!

Economic success, of course, is a relative matter whatever income class you are in—upper, middle, or lower (or even poverty). Finding a new job, getting a raise or promotion, or receiving the Employee of the Month Award, may or may not qualify as economic success. But obviously, millions of persons, families, and households are neither rich nor members of the upper middle class, but still consider themselves as economically successful. These may range from the retired married couple that has just bought the retirement home of their dreams because they worked hard and saved their money over the years for just this moment, to the single-parent mother who got a $1.00 an hour raise down at Wal-Mart's because she was such a good worker, to the young married couple that just graduated from law school and both landed jobs at a prestigious law firm. For all of these people, I would argue that what *ignited* them and sent them on their way to economic success was a sense of "hope and promise" about their economic futures.

This is because hope and promise are the essence of America. These two words act as the catalyst in a free market, capitalistic economy because they make wealth happen. Without them the system would not work. For all those who have experienced the hope and promise of America, therefore, let the celebration begin.

Remember the Rules of the Game

Human beings have all kinds of goals in life. Some want to be rich, some want to be happy, some want to raise a family, some want a clean environment—and some want all these things and more. But, if economic success, however one defines it, is your goal in life along with perhaps others, there are certain rules that must be kept in mind in a free market, capitalistic system.

These are rules that flow naturally from an economic order, such as the one we have in the United States. They are rules, unfortunately, that many people have forgotten—and, as a consequence, result in a lot of anxiety, grief, and complaint. They serve not only as rules but realities as to how our economic system operates. They won't necessarily guarantee economic success, but they'll help one understand why it may elude them.

Rule No. 1. Responsibility to Oneself

This is perhaps the most obvious rule of all, but the one that is, perhaps, violated the most in contemporary society. When we come into this world it is our parents (or parent or some adult) that are responsible for our well-being, and this they do for many years until we reach some stage in life when we are "on our own." Of course, today there are young adults still being cared for by their parents to various degrees.

Much is meant by "responsibility to oneself." Obviously, hygiene and grooming come naturally as does personal safety and…staying healthy. But, as is well-known, a lot of us really aren't very responsible when it even comes to our own health. How many of us could lose some weight or lower our blood pressure and cholesterol by stopping smoking and eating a better diet? But these are miniscule items relative to others on the pathway to economic success.

Let's begin with our home finances. How many have "run up" their charge cards to exorbitant amounts or figured the best way out of their debt was to file for bankruptcy? But then the response no doubt would become: "It's not my fault…it's the interest rates that are killing us…it's not fair…I need this and that…." So, in your mind, it's the department store and the auto dealer who *made* you buy all those things. What about health insurance for yourself and your family? Can't afford it you say, "'cause it's too expensive," but what about the plasma TV sitting on the rack over there? There's no point in dwelling on this for too long since it's so obvious that discipline (a means for achieving personal responsibility) is nowhere in sight in so many households today.

We can move onto the job or the workplace, a key to economic success—and we can ask the same kind of questions. Am I giving it my best effort? Could I do better? Did I earn my pay? All of us at one time or another wanted to stay home and call in on "sick leave" or take a longer lunch hour than we should have. But, in contemporary circles, "everybody does it." And what about our job skills and training? Is it my place to go off and get more training to make me more effective on the job or should I wait for the boss to send me? As we sit there, day after day, waiting for our time to retire, can we honestly say to ourselves that our employer got his money's worth? Or did I really take him for a ride…and besides he doesn't pay me enough!

Before we begin worrying about our *social responsibilities*, like participating in "this" charity event or contributing to "that" fund, perhaps many people should take a look in the mirror and see how they would honestly grade themselves on a test of *personal responsibility*. Many of these social concerns, of course, have that "fuzzy, feel good" return to them, while the personal concerns, the ones involving one's own responsibility simply have that "guilty, turn off" return. But, alas, so much of today's culture is permeated with the conscious-us attitude, something that must be eschewed, or at least placed in proper perspective.

As individuals brought into this world, and more importantly, into this nation blessed with its economic system and its wealth, we have a basic responsibility to oneself if we wish to be beneficiaries of our fortunate births.

Rule No. 2. Contributing to the Commonweal

Just because we were born here and raised into adulthood doesn't mean we are here for a free ride. It's hard to believe, but this is just what some people believe today.

Look around.

This rule, contributing something, of course, is related to the first rule. You do have a responsibility to contribute something—and this doesn't mean pitching in a five-dollar bill at church every Sunday or throwing a bundle of old clothes in the Salvation Army hopper. In a free market, capitalistic system, if you want economic remuneration, you have to contribute something, your skill, your time, your capital.

In the modern welfare states of Europe, and to some extent even in this country, many people expect that it is a "right" to have this and that provided to us. It is a right because we are citizens of such-and-such country so I expect my free health care and my five-week paid vacation every year. And in this country, how many of us have heard the cry that affordable housing, a college education, and freedom from hunger is a *right*—the justification being that, "It's my right because I'm a citizen."

Indeed, the first step in learning Rule No. 2. is realizing this: There is an important relationship between our contribution and our remuneration—positive and direct—the more you contribute the more you're remunerated—it's as simple as that! Naturally, there are all sorts of deviations from this standard that can be cited (e.g., the income of a teacher vs. that of a playboy heir), but just try denying the basic principle by contributing nothing and the point will become obvious.

Rule No. 3. Risks Are Everywhere

The beauty of the United States and its free market, capitalistic system is that it is filled with economic opportunities, but the harsh reality is that it is also filled with economic risks. Of course, no one likes risks; we always want the sure thing. The problem is that many of us have been lulled into the false notion that there are no risks, or shouldn't be, in this great, free land.

So the mainstream media love to bring attention to the risks and perils of economic life in America—it's their way of puncturing this balloon of "risk less" economic life. Low-wage work, dead-end jobs, downsizing, outsourcing, layoffs, unemployment, bankruptcy, poverty, and on and on—these are the deadly evils of capitalism, according to the media. Every night we can hear the frightening stories of the "middle class squeeze," the job cutbacks at Circuit City and Delphi and those ahead in the auto industry, the under-funded pensions, the skyrocketing level of personal bankruptcies, and the coming recession.

It should be obvious that if one totaled up the number of economic risks Americans have experienced throughout the nation's history and then totaled up the number of economic opportunities they've experienced that the latter would dwarf the former. Can we believe otherwise—as much as the elite media would have us do? Do we even have to consult the historical records on gross domestic product or national income?

But yes, the risks are there and so many people forget about them, put them out of their mind—and go on believing this job will last forever, or my pension is solid as a rock, or they'll never cut my hard-earned health benefits. Where was it written that when you took that job, it was yours for life or this was your ticket to the "golden years?" Would it have been better if there never had been that job in the first place, with its health insurance, and years of paid vacation and sick leave? Economic opportunity vs. economic risk in America—you can't have one without the other.

This Fertile Place...America

We live in a free and democratic nation. Its economy is based on free market capitalism. We are beholden to no other nation and tip our flag to none. If one is responsible to oneself, contributes something to society, and does not fear economic risk, this country is an economically fertile place.

Thousands and thousands of fortunes have been made in the United States over its lifetime and these fortunes have provided the basis of the nation's wealth today. But despite the nation's fecundity for wealth making, there is no formula, no system, no recipe for making wealth.[8] All that can be done is to make the conditions optimal for it to happen.

We all know of the real big fortunes like Henry Ford's, Andrew Carnegie's, and Bill Gates's, but consider those of other famous names, like Charles Goodyear and David Buick. Although Goodyear did produce a way of producing rubber for the auto industry, he died $200,000 in debt and Buick, founder of the Buick Motor Car Company, died in poverty.[9] And many of the "dot.com" fortunes of the late 1990s have melted away with the bursting of the bubble, just as they did during and after the Great Depression of the 1930s.

America's unusual capacity to produce wealth is very much like a garden, a fertile garden. In some years it produces bumper crops, in others the harvests are much less copious, but it always produces thanks to the vigilance of the gardener. Obviously, the garden sometimes produces a lot of weeds amongst the plants, choking and restraining the growth. They must be pulled and disposed of, somewhere away from the garden. The sick and unhealthy plants must be treated with insecticides or pulled out and uprooted too. The garden must be cultivated, its baked earth broken up so that the life enhancing rains can feed the shoots. Stones must be removed, piled high in the corner away from the spreading vines. And the most important of tasks for a bountiful harvest from the garden comes in making conditions right for growth—preparing the garden for plant-ing. It must be plowed and then fertilized, its soil smelling of life and fecundity, awaiting the seed. If the preparation is interrupted or done out of sequence, the future crop is jeopardized. And the garden must always be protected, fenced off from the pests that prey upon its ripening bounty. Wealth happens, but it happens only if conditions are right and the right things are done, just as with a garden.

Americans have been the most successful gardeners in the history of man because we made conditions right for the garden to grow and we did the right things to it. But there are always those who want to experiment, try something new, tinker with a new fertilizer or insecticide, or a new kind of garden tool. Some want to cut back the size of the garden so as to grow only what we need and others want to expand it into unknown patches of earth; some want to plant only one crop and others want to try a different crop in row after row. And still others say we should let the garden grow wild and forget it—and simply let it fill with wild flowers and the pests we've always wanted to keep away. Decisions concerning the garden are never ending—but Americans have always made the right ones, for the most part, and our national wealth is the evidence.

Forbes magazine does an excellent job each year in keeping track of America's richest 400 people. To get on the list the minimum size of one's net worth had to be in the neighborhood of $1 billion. They've been doing this for almost 25 years. In 2006 they reported that the "rich got richer" for the fourth consecutive year with the collective net worth of the nation's wealthiest 400 people rising by $120 billion to $1,250,000,000,000, or $1.25 trillion.[10] To put this figure in perspective, consider the following: according to the Board of Governors of the Federal Reserve System, in 2005 the net worth of all households and nonprofit organizations was $52.11 trillion.[11] In other words, this tiny fraction of people—just 400 out of a population of almost 300 million—owned 2.4 percent of every-thing in America.

Is this troubling? Should it be? Of course not. Just think of it the other way around. Were it not with the help of these 400 and their fortunes, would our collective net worth in this country be over the $50 trillion mark? I don't think so. So let them have their billions—and forget about Bill Gates ($53 billion net worth), Warren Buffett ($46 billion), the CEOs, and all the others in the top 1 percent.

But what do you say to the little guy, the guy who's about to lose his job or his health insurance or is besieged by mounting tuition bills, and credit card payments? Or a "real" little guy that *The New York Times* wrote about a couple of years ago—a 68-year-old retiree from Bethlehem Steel Company who lost his health care coverage and a third of his pension when the company went "belly up?"[12] According to the story, this retiree had 32 years of service with the company and the cuts in his benefits have a bitter taste in his mouth.

As much as you read and reread the article, you can't help feeling badly for this retiree—and especially when you find out he's had to get a job as a school cafeteria worker to make ends meet. There are always the extenuating circumstances: the company is now under new management, they're trying to cut costs, to stay competitive with foreign imports, to save the few thousands of jobs that are left in the industry, and on and on. But there's the retiree—is he another victim of our mean capitalists?

Other than having all the stockholders of the company cash in their stock and provide a superfund (which wouldn't probably last very long) for this retiree and all the others in his shoes, the answer is only cold and heartless. But it is the answer. It flows from the economic system our nation operates under: *No economic opportunity, without economic risk.* Unfortunate as this retiree's situation is, as well as the situations of the thousands of others like him, and the thousands of others who will eventually go through similar economic traumas in the years ahead when other "elder" industries like steel and autos run into financial difficulties, this answer is very blunt. As much as one would like a guarantee about one's economic future, there aren't any under free market capitalism—there never have been, and there never will be. The most that we can do, or our economic system can do, is provide some "cushion," or relief from the economic trauma that befell this man. As Chairman Bernanke of the Federal Reserve Board said (see Chapter 1), one of the bedrock principles of economic life in America is the provision of *insurance* against adverse economic outcomes—and over the decades our country has attempted to do this.

Yet, our economic history is replete with examples of fortunes lost, ways of life swept away in a flash, and descents into poverty. It's not that the present economic tragedies of Americans are a brand new experience, even though they appear that way in the media. We've read about the closing of the mill towns in New England, the westward trek of the Okies, the end of the Old South—over and over, as if these were the American legacies of its economic system. But no, we do know better—and as was said before, if we placed this nation's economic opportunities on one side of a scale and its economic risks on the other, the scale would tell us the truth. It's just that it's so hard to bear the economic heartbreaks.

I used to spend my winter months in a retirement community in the deep south. It wasn't a super-luxurious community, but it is gated, has a couple of golf courses and fitness centers. It is very middle class. Some of the residents are surely in the upper middle class, and a few are in the lower middle, but the vast majority are probably in the middle middle class. No doubt some have had, and are having, financial problems in their "senior years," but I would suspect the vast majority are very proud and very happy with their economic lives. They, too, grew wealth—and are also the beneficiaries of this fertile place.

Notes

1.   *The American Heritage Dictionary: Office Edition*, 4th Ed. (Boston: Houghton Mifflin Co., 2001), p. 648.
2.   Kevin Phillips, *Wealth and Democracy: A Political History of the American Rich* (New York: Broadway Books, 2002).
3.   *Ibid.*, p. 422.
4.   Back at the turn of the nineteenth to the twentieth century, Andrew Carnegie, John D. Rockefeller, and others were brought before the U.S. Industrial Commission on Trusts in connection with their various financial dealings. This was, of course, the great era of "trust busting" begun in President McKinley's administration and advanced by President Theodore Roosevelt and President Taft.
5.   The use of the term "anointed" was prompted from the title of a book by the economist Thomas Sowell, *The Vision of the Anointed* (New York: Basic Books, 1995). This book is a criticism of the modern liberal mindset of the last few decades and the social policies it led to.
6.   Between 1992 and 1993, the mean income (in 2004 dollars) of the top quintile of households had increased by 8.4 percent while the mean income (in 2004 dollars) of the lowest quintile declined by 1.0 percent, according to the U.S. Census Bureau, *Income, Poverty, and Health Insurance Coverage in the United States: 2004*, P60-229 (Washington, DC: USGPO, 2005), Table A-3, p. 40.
7.   These are terms that have been popularized in the outstanding book by Frank Levy and Richard J. Murnane, *The New Division of Labor: How Computers Are Creating the Next Job Market* (New York: Russell Sage Foundation, 2004).
8.   This, despite the many books and guides about achieving wealth, such as the popular book of the 1990s by Thomas J. Stanley and William D. Danko, *The Millionaire Next Door* (Marietta, GA: Longstreet Press, Inc., 1996) and the more recent contribution by Donald J. Trump and Robert T. Kiyosaki, *Why We Want You to Be Rich* (Rich Press, October, 2006).
9.   Michael Reynard, *Money Secrets of the Rich and Famous,* (New York: Allworth Press, 1999), p. xii.
10.   "America's 400 Richest," *Forbes*, (*http://www.forbes.com*), September 21, 2006.
11.   U.S. Census Bureau, *Statistical Abstract of the United States: 2007*, Washington, DC, 2007, No. 703, p. 464.

12.   Eduardo Porter, "Reinventing the Mill," *The New York Times*, October 22, 2005, pp. B1 and B5.

8

Good Inequality vs. Bad Inequality?

> *And don't be afraid to see what you see.*
> —Ronald Reagan

Several years ago, Finis Welch, a well-known economist wrote an article entitled, "In Defense of Inequality," in one of his profession's most highly respected journals.[1] In our popular culture, especially the media, such a title would represent a shocking display of insensitivity. To even suggest that inequality could be defended would be considered arrogance of the meanest variety. For an economics journal whose audience is primarily economists, however, the title was not shocking at all, only eye-catching.

The article's main thrust was to demonstrate that inequality in recent years was getting a "bum rap," or as the author put it, "…inequality is an economic 'good' that has received too much bad press."[2] As an illustration, the author of the article went on to show that despite the upward trend in wage inequality (he was writing at the end of the 1990s), the much lamented earnings gap between women and men in the work force had closed considerably in recent years.

I will mention, explicitly, the beneficial effect of income inequality: Incentives. If it weren't for the people who had achieved (and were achieving) economically more than oneself, who would one look up to as their role models or the, "I want to be like…," person or persons? Emulation is a natural component of the human spirit, and incentives are important for any society. After all, how boring it would be if everyone had the same income, and lived in the same kind of house, and drove the same kind of car.

So, it might just be that in all the media frenzy about the "yawning" income gap, we have been looking at things the wrong way. Indeed, it will be argued in this chapter that…*growing income inequality can come in*

149

two varieties, the good kind and the bad kind, and in the past, we've been experiencing a dose of the former. This good kind of inequality can flow as naturally from our nation's economic system as the bad kind—and it is vitally important that we recognize the difference. By not recognizing this difference, we potentially jeopardize those in search of the American Dream and those who have found it. By not recognizing this difference, the mainstream media has misled you.

Economic policies, such as tax cuts, trade agreements, and Federal spending decisions, designed for helping Americans to reach that Dream, of course, are at the heart of the national debate between the political left and right. Over the last few decades the issue of tax cuts, and especially so those for the rich, have created the most heated discussions.

This issue was a derivative of the "supply side" school of economics, which grew in popularity with President Reagan's administration. Although eschewed by many economists as a legitimate macroeconomic theory, it certainly challenged the "received" theory associated most often with the famous British economist John Maynard Keynes. Ever since the Great Depression, the belief had been that stimulating the "demand side" of the economy (i.e., consumer spending) was the best way of promoting economic growth. But the economic malaise of the 1970s, which was characterized by high unemployment and inflation (i.e., stagflation), seriously brought into question this Keynesian-inspired economic policy. With the ascendancy of the Republicans in the 1980s and the Reagan tax cuts, supply side economics had become the favored way of growing the economy. The new fiscal mantra of the Federal government had become, "cut taxes, raise revenues." Consequently, when the left-leaning critics rant and rave about income inequality and how it has grown over the last thirty years or so, it is also the economic policies of the "supply siders" that they are implicitly inveighing against.[3]

The argument over the theoretical legitimacy of supply side economics vis-à-vis demand side economics can be put aside for another day. The essential point for this discussion is that contained in the former is a tiny, glistening "nugget" of human truth, a truth that even Keynes himself recognized. George Gilder, a proponent of supply side economics in the early 1980s, wrote extensively about Keynes's recognition of this.[4] According to Gilder, who was paraphrasing Keynes, it was simply "daring acts of entrepreneurship" (i.e., investment) that led to greater aggregate demand (i.e., consumption) in Keynes's world. In other words, whether the theory is supply side or demand side, it is that intangible desire to pursue one's self-interest that makes the economy grow.

It is because of this tiny "nugget"—and the damage that can be done to it—that the nation must seriously rethink the income gap. As this book has demonstrated, the desire to bury this nugget under false social fears and untoward rhetoric is dangerous for the economic future of the nation. Indeed, the nugget must be protected and perfected.

Distinguishing between "Good" and "Bad" Inequality

It was shown in Chapter 2 *how* the income gap widened over recent decades—basically, as a result of an upward expansion in the upper half of the income distribution. Everyone's before-tax money incomes rose over these decades, but those with the higher incomes rose the fastest. The reason *why* this happened, according to most economists, was that "premiums" were being paid to persons with the greatest skills and productivity.

Some observers of this development concluded that the nation's economy had turned into a meritocracy. Those on the "far left" viewed the development with alarm because, in their view, the less talented and less endowed members of society were being penalized for their defi-ciencies. How could this growing income gap occur in a country based on such noble principles like that of equality? The counterargument, of course, was this: Should the talented and skilled, whose incomes rose the fastest, be penalized for their economic success instead? How could this be justified in a country founded on another noble principle—economic freedom? And so, we have an apparent ethical conundrum.

As was also mentioned in Chapter 2, the Pareto criterion has fre-quently been called upon to free us from ethical thickets such as these.[5] Again, this criterion says that any economic change can be considered good for general welfare if at least someone is made better off (in an economic sense) and no one is made worse off. Table 2.1 in Chapter 2 displayed the changes that took place in the average annual before-tax money incomes (adjusted for inflation) of households by quintiles of the income distribution between 1967 and 2006. From the lowest to the highest income quintile, average income had risen—by 38 percent for the lowest quintile to 83 percent for the highest (the rise in income in the second quintile was the smallest—26 percent—of all quintiles). Accord-ing to the Pareto criterion, then, this would represent an improvement in economic welfare—and since inequality had risen over this period, this could be considered a dose of "good" growing income inequality. On the other hand, if over this period, the real household incomes of the bottom quintile, for example, had fallen by 38 percent while the highest had gone up by 83 percent, this would have been a dose of "bad" growing income inequality.

Many observers from the political left (and even some from the middle) argue that with the continued existence of poverty in America, this income growth pattern of recent years is only exacerbating economic class divisions. Their point is well-taken. There should be no poverty in America—but the economic freedoms of others should not be constrained either.

Furthermore, one must consider a couple of extenuating circumstances involving poverty statistics. First, the incidence of poverty, as discussed earlier, has changed little over the last few decades according to the Census Bureau (in 2006 the poverty rate was 12.3 percent and in 1967 it was 14.2 percent).[6] Second, the poverty definition, as discussed in Appendix A, has been the subject of much criticism over these many years for a number of reasons (such as the fact that the definition is based on a ratio of food expenditures to total household expenditures that was established decades ago and that the income definition used in the survey of household incomes is a very narrow one and does not include in-kind income, for example, food stamps).

Because of the problems with the Census Bureau's poverty data, and to some extent its income data (see Appendix A for a more complete discussion), many economists, policy makers, and even the media, rely on other sources of income statistics for their analyses. One source is the income data developed by the economists of the government's Congressional Budget Office (CBO). By using different statistical techniques and sources, they are able to build upon the census money income concept. They add to the Census income data the capital gains received by households, their employer contributions to health insurance plans and retirement plans, the value of Medicare and Medicaid insurance coverage as well as other government transfer programs such as food stamps and housing subsidies. Then they subtract from these income statistics estimates of individual households' Federal income tax liabilities as well as their payroll taxes, excise taxes, and even the corporate tax liability that would be passed on to any household who earned interest or dividends. CBO uses this information in their work for Congress. The assumption is that these data are a "comprehensive" picture of the after-tax incomes of American households.

References to the CBO income data have frequently been seen in the media in connection with the income gap. Typically, the item that catches everyone's eye is the skyrocketing growth of real after-tax household incomes at the very top of the income distribution—the top 1 percent—compared to the much slower growth for households below them. But what is less frequently shown by the media, and what confirms the cruder Census Bureau data, is that real household income increased in *each* income quintile of the income distribution over recent decades.

The CBO data in Table 8.1 are real after-tax income averages for each quintile of the distribution over the 1980-82 period and the 2000-2002 period.[7] There is no mistaking that the after-tax incomes of the top quintile of households did increase rapidly over this twenty-year period. The average income of this quintile expanded from $86,000 to $138,000, or 60 percent. This compares to the bottom quintile where real after-tax incomes moved up from $12,400 to $14,300, or only 15 percent. Real incomes also moved upward and faster in the next three higher income quintiles. In other words, using the most comprehensive income data that the government produces, the income changes that took place in the closing two decades of the twentieth century passed the Pareto criterion indicative of an improvement in overall economic welfare. This was a period of "good" growing income inequality.

But, of course, the elite media and left-of-center social commentators would say that these are simply statistics being evaluated on the

Table 8.1
Average Comprehensive After-Tax Annual Income (in 2002 dollars) of Households by Quintiles of the Income Distribution, 1980-82 and 2000-02*

Qunitile	2000-02	1980-82	Percent change
All Quintiles	$57,367	$41,300	38.9
Lowest	14,167	12,367	14.6
2nd	30,267	25,300	19.6
3rd	43,933	36,233	21.3
4th	61,833	48,167	28.4
Highest	137,867	86,133	60.1

Source: Congressional Budget Office

* Comprehensive after-tax income includes all cash income plus noncash income such as the value of food stamps, health insurance benefits, Medicare, and Medicaid, minus Federal individual income taxes, social insurance taxes, corporate income taxes, and Federal excise taxes.

basis of one economist's view as to what represents an improvement in a society's economic welfare. Indeed, they would say that the statistics are clear evidence of social inequality because not everyone is receiving an equal share of the growing income pie. But is that truly the case? From what we know of the productive capacities (e.g., their contribution to the economy) of each of these quintiles, their income growth rates were most likely commensurate with their contributions to the economy. Economic welfare had improved according to the CBO data, just as with the Census data.

Despite this confirmation of a "good" growing income inequality, the growth of income inequality, and the economic policies that presumably produced it, has permeated the nation's intelligentsia to such an extent that some of our most brilliant economists continue to dismiss this economic success. In his book, *The Roaring Nineties*, Joseph E. Stiglitz, a Nobel Prize winning economist, criticized the Reagan administration for following a policy of trickle-down economics which Stiglitz called "widely discredited." He wrote: "Those at the bottom saw their incomes actually fall in real terms during the two decades from 1973 to 1993."[8] I find this to be misleading, especially if he was referring to changes in real average household incomes of the lowest quintile of the income distribution over that time period.[9]

The legacy of supply side economics and its impact on economic welfare will be the subject of countless doctoral dissertations and scholarly papers in the realm of economics for years to come. Whether or not it is a legitimate economic theory, at the same level of Keynes's macroeconomic theory, is not to be decided here. Rather, its import is for what lies at its core, much like Keynes theory. It is that part of the human spirit that is buried deep within each and every one of us, "self-interest."

A Different "Trickle Down"

The *idea* that economic behavior motivated on the basis of one's self-interest will eventually lead to overall economic growth and prosperity blossomed a few centuries ago in the writings of Adam Smith. In his opening chapter of *The Wealth of Nations,* Smith discusses the productive power of the division of labor, or the specialization of labor. It came about as a result of man's "...propensity to truck, barter, and exchange one thing for another." And the commonweal was best served (through greater output) if everyone was allowed to do this; interfere with it and the consequences would be ruinous. Clearly, modern day manifestations of this idea can be seen to various degrees in the calls for free and unfettered markets, laissez faire economics, free trade, tax cuts, and so forth, on the part of conservative economists and those on the political right.

Embodied in these manifestations of the fundamental idea of economic self-interest is that everyone will benefit in the process via the "market." For example, reductions in corporate and individual income taxes presumably will encourage greater investment in capital assets (e.g., factories, mines, machinery), increased saving, and greater work effort, which ultimately will lead to more jobs and greater production. In other words, the money that does not have to be paid in taxes can be used for investment and productive purposes and encourage people to work even more. Obviously, not every one nor every corporation uses these dollars and incentives in a "productive" sense. But many will, and especially those who have that little, glistening nugget inside them—the ones who see the opportunities to make more money and more profits.

This, of course, happens not only when taxes are cut, but also when restrictions on trade are lifted, when new markets are opened, and when other measures are taken to expand economic freedoms. New economic opportunities arise—and given man's natural instinct of satisfying his economic self-interest, these opportunities will be seized upon in many instances.

Peter Jay, the former British Ambassador to the United States, made an interesting observation about man's basic desires in his book, *The Wealth of Man*. He wrote in the early pages that perhaps only more compelling a story than man's desire to survive in this world was his craving for wealth and "…material betterment."[10] Given this natural human instinct of wanting to improve one's lot in life *but* also given mankind's wide range of skills, talents, and dispositions (i.e., from those with little ability and ambition to those with much), not everyone will avail themselves of these new economic opportunities to the same extent. As a consequence, an inequality of outcomes will occur.

And this is "where" and "why" the "trickle down effect" I speak of begins. From the wide range of human beings with different skills, talents, and dispositions, economic self-interest becomes translated into different economic behaviors. Some people imbued with much ability and ambition will become entrepreneurial, others with lesser endowments will be engaged in enterprises of a lesser entrepreneurial nature, and so on down the distribution of human abilities and ambitions, to eventually those who have the least endowments. It is from the very first category of human beings that the initial "trickle" begins, only to be moved on by others with lesser endowments, because this trickle is interpreted to be in their economic self-interest to keep passing on. The result is wealth. Therefore, the human process of trickle down flows directly from man's differential capabilities to engage in economic activity.

This is why many conservative economists are not necessarily appalled by wealth and income gaps. Indeed, such inequalities are a characteristic of dynamic free market economies. As Ludwig von Mises, one of the nation's pre-eminent economic thinkers wrote over fifty years ago, "Inequality of wealth and incomes is the cause of the masses' well-being, not the cause of anybody's distress."[11] To which might be added, as long as the "nugget" is preserved and protected.

The astute reader by now should see that the "trickle down" being elaborated upon here is different than what we read or hear about in the media and even academia. The political left and far left Democrats, of course, often refer to Republican tax cut proposals and other supply side economic policies as, "mere trickle down." The popular interpretation of trickle down, consequently, carries a negative connotation with it—and implies that what benefits the rich and wealthy will eventually trickle down to the little guy. This is *not* what is meant here. Rather, it means each member of society who acts upon their economic self-interest to the best of their ability and ambition—adds to the trickle.

Despite the absence of an elaborate economic theory and empirical testing of the process, in reality this is nothing more than common sense. Consider the building of the medieval cathedrals of Europe. These were financed largely by the church and its wealthy patrons and, of course, they were built by craftsmen and laborers, who then went out and passed along their part of the "trickle" to others. Fast forward to today. Look about our nation and see cities like New York and Chicago, skyscrapers reaching upward to the sky. They all began with someone, somewhere, sometime ago, who provided the financing (capital), which was then passed (i.e., trickled) on to the architects, engineers, and construction workers who built the buildings, which in turn began to create more wealth from the rents and leases they produced—trickle by trickle by trickle.

Across this sweep of time, of course, the resulting advance in human well-being has gone through its fits and starts, as Peter Jay suggests.[12] In his book, he also summarizes this advance with a poignant observation by referencing two of the greatest thinkers of the last 300 years, Charles Darwin and Adam Smith:

> The driving forces have been the natural selection of innovations that work and the invisible hand that, under the right conditions, channels private appetite into attain-

ment of social ends or at least of widely shared advantage. Both are ethically blind, indifferent alike to individual happiness and social justice.[13]

Despite the enormous economic gaps between the wealthiest nations of the world and the poorest, the economic progress of mankind is undeniable. In the most prosperous of nations, such as the United States, society has been very cognizant of the "ethical blindness" of the natural selection of innovations and the workings of the invisible hand. Simply look at our law books and the social and economic policies that protect us from these innovations and the invisible hand, or as might be said, free market capitalism. (Indeed, one could easily argue that our economic system is really a "modified" version of free market capitalism.) No, our nation is not ethically blind to individual happiness and social justice, but neither is it blind to incursions upon individual liberties and economic freedoms.

Americans are a proud people. But despite that pride we like to blend in and feel that we're just as good as the next guy—even though, deep down, we know that's not true, not when it comes to certain attributes. We know there are rich people, or people richer than us, people who have great skills in making money, people who work harder than we do, people who have outachieved us economically. We typically don't like to talk about such things. But, it really shouldn't bother us. We should celebrate their success because they have added to the trickle—just as we have in our own way.

Bill Gates, Warren Buffett, Donald Trump, and all the other super economic achievers will always be around in a free market, capitalistic system. This is the way the system works. We are all part of the tickle down process—and the best evidence of this has been America's middle class revolutions, the first one and the second one that is still going on. It should comfort us that the trickle down process continues to work and that the little nugget buried inside each and every one of us continues to glisten.

Beware of Those Income Gap Stories

This short book, of course, will not change the course of national events nor the attitudes some Americans have about their country and its economic system. But it may start some readers to pause and begin rethinking the income gap.

More will be heard about the income gap in the days ahead, without a doubt. The mainstream media know a good story when they see one—the "victim-culprit" angle appeals to one's conscience. The story speaks to our sense of fairness, justice, and even basic morality, and all of us want to be known as fair, just, and moral individuals. Consider some of these past news stories.

Robert Reich, President Clinton's former Secretary of Labor, wrote a thoughtful op-ed piece in *The New York Times*, which summarizes the situation many Americans find themselves in these days—struggling with the many ethical and quasi-ethical economic issues that confront us.[14] It was about Wal-Mart. As a liberal, he deplores the supposedly low wages and benefit package that Wal-Mart provides its employees, but at the same time, and unlike most other liberals, he admits he likes the low prices the company offers him and other consumers. His point is, however, that instead of having the knock-down, drag-out fight between those who want the low consumer prices and those who want better quality jobs, why can't there be a compromise on both sides of the issue—perhaps sacrificing, and living with somewhat higher consumer prices for somewhat better paying jobs.

It's an appealing plea of Mr. Reich's, but unfortunately it won't work. It won't work because Wal-Mart would soon be losing customers to Target or some other competitor—and besides, the 1.4 million employees of Wal-Mart must see something in these jobs as was mentioned earlier in Chapter 1. No, Mr. Reich is simply wrestling with the cold reality of the market place—like many other Americans.

In the same vein, a front page story appeared in *The Wall Street Journal* with a headline "made to scare" and tug at the sentimental heartstrings of its readers. It was about the automobile industry and the rough days the automakers and their suppliers are having in the face of stiffer foreign competition and higher gasoline prices—all of which is threatening workers' jobs, or as the headline read, "A Middle Class Made by Detroit Is Now Threatened by Its Slump."[15] This wasn't a prescriptive story like Mr. Reich's piece. It just went on about how the paychecks and benefit packages of various workers were being cut and how the economic futures of their households were now in jeopardy. These were very difficult situations—a "putting-yourself-in-their-shoes" type of narrative.

Again, the story plucks at the conscience, even for those who believe in free markets. What kind of system is this where you're making $65 an hour and they (management) want to cut your pay in half? Something's wrong! We need wage insurance! We need another system!

These are some of the conclusions one can draw from such a story. But another conclusion is this: as difficult and cold-hearted as it sounds, this is free market capitalism at work—this is its savage side. Just as it had its beneficent side and produced a $65 an hour job, so, too, it can take it away—"opportunity and risk" is how the game is played—even though our economic system has attempted to minimize risk and soften the economic misfortunes.

These two stories from the media were recounted so as to remind you, the reader, why we must all *rethink* the income gap. It is very obvious that the free market, capitalistic system has been under attack for many years. The attack has been pushed along by many major media outlets—and would have never materialized without them. No wonder the body politic has class and inequality on its mind when the nations premiere newspaper, *The New York Times,* advertises its own book written by its own correspondents entitled *Class Matters* with the lead advertising line questioning, "Is the American Dream Just a Dream?"[16] All of this in the year 2005 when the nation's unemployment rate was hovering around the 5.0 percent mark, average monthly job growth was about 250,000 jobs, the nation's gross domestic product was growing at an annual rate of 3.5 percent, and the incidence of poverty was not much different than it was 30 years ago.[17]

Perhaps no other economic development of the past 50 years has done more to frighten our society and polarize it than the widening income gap. Economic problems have occurred in the past and will occur in the future and they will be dealt with as they always have. The greatness of America has been its willingness to negotiate and compromise with one another—and then get on with it. Ever since this nation's Civil War, the representatives of business and labor, ranchers and farmers, miners and mine owners, dock workers and ship owners, and all the other disparate representatives of economic agents across this country have worked out their differences. Even throughout the Great Depression when the unemployed were standing in bread lines and the political left was toying with communism, economic differences were resolved, and the nation moved on, in many ways changed, but in others, very much the same. So, there is no point, today, in pitting one class against another, one who is the victim and one who is the culprit, which is the bottom line implication of much of today's income gap rhetoric.

Indeed, this divisive rhetoric, and its negative implications, reached new heights with the occurrence of, of all things, a meteorological event. In late August of 2005, a devastating hurricane slammed into the Gulf Coast states of Mississippi and Louisiana. Hurricane Katrina caused billions of dollars of damage and hundreds of deaths. But its aftermath—the breaking of the levees of New Orleans and subsequent flooding of the city—was the news that transfixed the nation. The images of people waving for help from atop their flooded homes, and the crowds of flood victims lingering outside the city's Superdome and Coliseum waiting for help, stunned the nation's conscience. Where was the help?

We all know the tales of recrimination that then transpired—it's the Governor's fault, the Mayor screwed-up, the President is on vacation—and finally these stories lost their traction in the daily press, as most things eventually do. But in amongst the criticism and finger-pointing there was also commentary from our politicians about the obvious social and economic inequities that Katrina had uncovered. The income gap had emerged, once again—in the aftermath of a hurricane.[18]

But the impact of Hurricane Katrina on the income gap rhetoric, of course, did not end there. *The New York Times* ran a lengthy story featuring the "chasm" that existed between the Katrina-related economic hardships of "have and have-not" families. One line read:

> …the poorest have turned desperately destitute, while the well-to-do make do with what they have left.[19]

The "class-consciousness twist" to the story could not be missed. What did the reporter of this story expect to find—the opposite of the obvious? That the poorest households were flourishing and the well-to-do households were floundering? Or, was the point of the story *really* something else: to keep the "haves and have-nots" and the unfairness of economic life in America on the front page?

To write such commentary on the misfortunes of hurricane victims was, in my opinion, unnecessary—and making a political point at the expense of their *(all of them)* suffering. The vast majority of America's citizens know that poverty and poor people exist in this nation and that for those in New Orleans, Katrina was a devastating blow. To state the obvious was only an attempt to perpetuate the income gap muddle.

We have heard how divided our nation has become in recent years. There have always been differences between the major political parties of the country, but they appear as far apart as they ever have been on the major issues confronting the nation, such as the war in Iraq, abortion rights, Supreme Court appointees, and economic policy. The so-called "culture war" rages, at least on the radio and TV talk shows, and issues like the environment and global warming, gay marriage, school prayer, creationism, and on and on, all get tossed about like balls in a juggling act. Demonstrations for animal rights, protests over smoking in bars and restaurants, and picket-lines in front of abortion clinics sweep on and off our TV screens of the evening news shows—and we are pulled into the culture war, asked to choose up sides. Then, with eyes glazed over, we listen to a news anchor report on about a compensation package for a CEO from a large corporation that was just negotiated, and the widening income gap.

Perhaps this nation's culture war got its start when the first news about growing income inequality reached the airwaves. After all, news about those "with a lot" and "with little" sets the mind to thinking about many things that one feels strongly about—the victim vs. culprit paradigm. We do know that after the pronouncements of the politicians and the mainstream media concerning Hurricane Katrina, there was a 10 percent increase in the proportion of Americans who believed that this is a have and have-not nation.[20] The point is that the media and their "news" of the income gap has an impact on public opinion.

Words can be powerful. This is why the media chose to use *income gap* in their headlines instead of *income inequality*. The former has come to mean social polarization and social exclusion. The latter, on the other hand, means income differences and has a statistical ring. One is loaded with accusation, the other with curiosity.

As we move further into the twenty-first century and have a look around the economic landscape of America, it would behoove everyone to be mindful of this difference. It's critical for the nation's future.

Is what we see the result of a "good" inequality or a "bad" inequality? Is our perception of the economic scene consistent with its reality? Have we been misled? Have we overlooked the second middle class revolution?

Notes

1.   Finis Welch, "In Defense of Inequality" (The Richard T. Ely Lecture), *The American Economic Review*, May 1999, pp. 1-17.
2.   *Ibid.*
3.   At least two liberal economists suggest, however, that there may have been some "mild" beneficial affects on the economy as a result of economic policies derived from the supply side school of economics during President Reagan's administrations. See Robert Heilbroner and Lester Thurow, *Economics Explained (Revised and Updated)* (New York: Simon and Schuster Inc., 1994), pp. 126-127.
4.   George Gilder, *Wealth and Poverty* (New York: Basic Books, Inc., Publishers, 1981), pp. 31-44.
5.   See the section in Chapter 2 entitled, "Pausing for Pareto…and the Poor."
6.   *Income, Poverty, and Health Insurance Coverage in the United States: 2006* (P60-233), U. S. Bureau of the Census, HHES Division (Washington, DC: USGPO, August 2006), Table B-1, p. 44.

7.   *Historical Effective Federal Tax Rates: 1979-2002*, Congressional Budget Office, March 2005, Table 1C.
8.   Joseph E. Stiglitz, *The Roaring Nineties* (New York: W.W. Norton & Company, Inc., 2003), p. 286.
9.   According to Census Bureau data for the years 1973 and 1993, real average incomes in each quintile had increased. See *Income, Poverty, and Health Insurance Coverage in the United States: 2005* (P60-231), Table A-3, pp. 40-41.
10.   Peter Jay, *The Wealth of Man* (New York: Public Affairs, 2000), p. ix.
11.   Ludvig von Mises, "Inequality of Wealth and Incomes," *Ideas and Liberty*, The Foundation for Economic Education, 1955.
12.   Peter Jay, *The Wealth of Man* (New York: Public Affairs, 2000), p. xii.
13.   *Ibid.*
14.   Robert B. Reich, "Don't Blame Wal-Mart," *The New York Times*, February 28, 2005, p. A25.
15.   Jeffrey McCracken, "A Middle Class Made by Detroit Is Now Threatened by Its Slump," *The Wall Street Journal*, Nov. 14, 2005, pp. A1 and A8.
16.   *The New York Times,* November 13, 2005, p. 16.
17.   These data were based on monthly and quarterly averages obtained from the Web site, *http://www.fedstats.gov*.
18.   *The New York Times*, September 13, 2005, p. A16.
19.   Jodi Wilgoren, "In Tale of Two Families, A Chasm Between Haves and Have-Nots," *The New York Times,* September 5, 2005, pp. A1 and A10.
20.   "Katrina Relief Effort Raises Concerns Over Excessive Spending, Waste," The Pew Research Center for the People and the Press, Oct. 19, 2005, at *http://www. people-press.org*. According to the Pew Research Center survey of nearly 1,500 respondents in October 2005, 48 percent believed that this was a "have-have not" nation, compared to 38 percent in March 2005.

Appendix A
Income Data and Other Related Issues

Most of the income data discussed in this book have been obtained from the Current Population Survey (CPS), a household survey of about 100,000 households, conducted by the Census Bureau. It is a monthly survey primarily used to collect employment and unemployment information for the U.S. Bureau of Labor Statistics. The CPS has been the source of annual income information for the nation on an annual basis ever since 1947.

Collecting Income Statistics with the CPS

In March of every year, Census Bureau enumerators ask, in addition to questions about employment and unemployment in the previous month, questions relating to a household's money income received in the preceding calendar year. These latter questions are referred to as the Annual Social and Economic Supplement. In other words, in March of 2007, CPS enumerators were asking questions concerning the incomes of each person, age fifteen years and over, in calendar year 2006.

The income concept used by the Census Bureau is a "money" income concept. This means that it relates to cash income, exclusive of capital gains, received before payment of personal income taxes, Social Security taxes, union dues, etc. By definition, therefore, the value of noncash governmental benefits like food stamps, health benefits, and subsidized housing are not included, nor is the value of employer-provided benefits, such as health insurance premiums, contributions to retirement plans, and educational and transportation expenses. This is an important conceptual distinction when comparing CPS income statistics to those of the Bureau of Economic Analysis (BEA) and the Internal Revenue Service (IRS), for example, because BEA and IRS utilize broader income concepts.

The CPS sample of households covers the fifty states and the District of Columbia (but excludes Puerto Rico and other outlying areas). It is, therefore, a nationally representative sample of the country's population.

The income estimates are controlled to national population estimates by age, race, sex, and Hispanic origin and to state population estimates by age obtained from the 2000 Decennial census. People living in institutions such as prisons, nursing homes, and long-term care facilities are not eligible to be interviewed, but military personnel living in a household with one other civilian (either on post or off) are eligible to be interviewed.

Because the CPS is essentially a probability sample of households, the income estimates are subject to both sampling error and nonsampling error. Sampling error occurs simply because a sample rather than a complete enumeration of all households was conducted, while nonsampling error occurs because of various problems associated with administering the survey, such as the nonresponse to certain income questions on the part of household respondents and errors committed in the handling of the data. In addition, for income questions that are not responded to, imputations of missing income data are made based on the income information of persons with similar demographic characteristics. The Census Bureau publishes standard errors for many of their major income estimates.[1] For example, the standard error on median household income in 2006 of $48,201 was ± $207.

For purposes of assessing long-run trends in income and earnings, the Census Bureau adjusts its estimates for changes in consumer prices, or inflation. It uses the BLS's experimental Consumer Price Index (CPI-U-RS) for the period from 1977 to 2006, and the Census Bureau derived the CPI-U-RS for years before 1977 by applying the 1977 CPI-U-RS-to-CPI-U ratio to the 1947 to 1976 CPI-U. Constant, or real, dollar income estimates are usually identified in the text of this book and have been either taken directly from Census Bureau publications (or their Web page) or derived by using other versions of the BLS's CPI for years before 1947.

One of the greatest challenges for income statisticians is collecting accurate and reliable income information for both ends of the income distribution, that is, the rich and the poor. Households at both ends of the distribution have traditionally been known for underreporting their incomes for a number of reasons, such as, forgetfulness, poor records, and more generally, reluctance to divulge income sources and their amounts. In other cases, complete nonresponse to the income questions by respondents from these households is occasionally experienced by CPS enumerators. Obviously, the underreporting of income at both ends of the income distribution is problematic for poverty and income inequality measurement.

Poverty Measurement

The CPS income statistics serve as the basis for the Federal government's official statistics on poverty in the nation. Families and unrelated individuals are classified as poor if their CPS annual money income in the previous year falls below various poverty thresholds defined on the basis of age, size of family, and other characteristics. These thresholds were originally established (and updated for inflation each year) by the Social Security Administration in 1964 and revised by Federal Interagency Committees in 1969 and 1980.

The thresholds are based on a 1961 Economy Food Plan developed by the Department of Agriculture in 1961, which reflect the different consumption requirements of families based on their size and composition. For example, the poverty threshold for a four-person family with two related children under 18 years of age in 2006 was $20,444; for a two-person family with one child under 18 in which the head of the household was under 65, the threshold was $13,896; and for a one-person household, in which the head was age 65 or older, the threshold was $9,669.[2]

Perhaps no other Federal government statistics have received as much criticism from various political and nonpolitical organizations as the Census Bureau's poverty statistics. Some of the criticisms are that the poverty thresholds are too low and they are based on dated and unrealistic consumption requirements; other criticisms of the thresholds center on the fact that the income data they are compared against (CPS annual money income) do not account for noncash benefits that poor families and individuals receive, such as food stamps, public housing, and Medicaid.

Because of many of these criticisms, the Census Bureau has presented, from time to time, experimental poverty estimates, which take into account the criticisms. These experimental estimates are developed using various estimating procedures, which yield synthetic values that are then added to the data obtained in the CPS. The Bureau released a report in July 1999 showing the effects of various experimental measures of poverty based on recommendations of a National Academy of Sciences panel that examined the government's poverty definition. The Office of Management and Budget (OMB), which makes the ultimate decision regarding how poverty is defined, however, has never acted upon these recommendations.

Income Inequality Measurement

The Census Bureau also publishes a variety of income inequality measures each year, as was mentioned in the text.[3] They vary from the simple to the complex. One of the principal measures the Bureau relies upon, and that is relied upon extensively in the academic literature, is the Gini index of income concentration. This index is based on the Lorenz curve, a graphical depiction (as shown in the figure) of the relationship between the percentage of all household income received by households (using the vertical axis) and the percentage of all households ranked from those with the lowest incomes to the highest (using the horizontal axis). In other words, one finds, according to the Census Bureau data on annual money income of households, that in 2006, the richest 20 percent of households in the nation received 50.5 percent of all money income.[4] The Lorenz curve, devised by Max O. Lorenz in 1905, was first used in a statistical paper relating to the measurement of wealth concentration.

With the help of the Lorenz curve, the Italian mathematician Corrado Gini formulated the Gini index. What his formula did was estimate the "area" that existed between the diagonal line in a square-shaped graph (in the context of the Lorenz curve, this means the same percentage of total money income is received by the same percentage of total households) and the Lorenz curve (which shows the true relationship between what percentage of total money income is received by what proportion of total households). In the Figure this would be the area, A, divided by the sum of area A and area B (the area below the Lorenz curve). Perfect

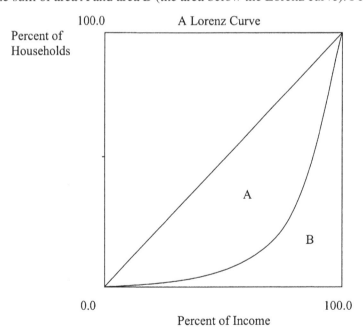

100.0   A Lorenz Curve

Percent of
Households

A

B

0.0   100.0

Percent of Income

income equality, therefore, would have a Gini index value of 0.0 and perfect income inequality would have a value of 1.0. In 2006, the Gini index for all households in the nation was .470.[5]

The Federal government has no "official" measure of income inequality. The Census Bureau, however, has historically featured changes in the Gini index, shares of income received by each quintile of the income distribution, and percentile ratios of annual money income for assessing changes in income inequality. As indicated in the text, the amount of change is sensitive to the measure being examined.

Income Statistics from the Congressional Budget Office (CBO)

To provide Congress with the most useful statistical information on the effect of various Federal taxes on household incomes, the CBO takes the basic CPS income statistics collected by the Census Bureau each year and enhances them in various ways.[6] In general, they attempt to broaden the Census Bureau's before tax money income concept and then take into account the affect of various Federal taxes that households are liable.

CBO uses a multi-step methodology with data from both the CPS and the Statistics of Income from the Internal Revenue Service (IRS). Through a statistical matching process of records from both sources, as well as regression analyses, CBO is able to create income records for various demographic groups, which contain information on not only cash or money income items (e.g., wages and salaries, interest, dividends, pensions) but also capital gains, the values of noncash income items (e.g., food stamps, employer-provided health insurance, Medicare, Medicaid), and the tax liabilities that would be incurred for four Federal taxes (i.e., individual income taxes, corporate income taxes, payroll taxes, and excise taxes).

Obviously, the CBO methodology is complicated and involves other manipulations and adjustments not mentioned here. But from the database created Congress is provided with important insights into the role of Federal taxes on the nation's household income distribution, and especially the effective Federal tax rates households are confronted with.

The after-Federal tax household income estimates produced by CBO provide another set of data by which to assess the economic well-being of American households as was discussed in the text. The CBO income estimates and their trends over time can differ, of course, from those obtained from the CPS of the Census Bureau. A case in point was in the opening years of this century, specifically, between 2000 and 2005. The text table below shows the percent changes in the Census Bureau's real average household income by income quintile and the CBO's real average after-Federal tax household income by quintile.

	Percent Change	
	Census	CBO
All Quintiles	-2.2	4.3
Lowest	-8.5	-1.3
2nd	-4.8	2.7
3rd	-3.3	5.7
4th	-2.2	4.8
Highest	-1.1	7.4

Although the two income measures are not directly comparable (e.g., one is after-tax and the other is before-tax), the CBO percent changes in real after-Federal tax income are considerably more sanguine than those of the Census estimates of real before-tax income between 2000 and 2005. No doubt this reflects to some extent the changes in the tax laws that were made in the earlier years of the decade. As will be recalled, much was made of the lack of income growth for American households (based on the Census data) during these years in the 2008 Presidential campaign.

Notes

1. See the various tables contained in *Income, Poverty, and Health Insurance Coverage in the United States: 2006*, P60-233, U.S. Bureau of the Census, HHES Division (Washington, DC: USGPO, August 2007).
2. *Ibid.*, p. 43.
3. *Ibid.*, Table A-3, pp. 38-39.
4. *Ibid.*
5. *Ibid.*
6. For a brief description of the CBO data, see *Historical Effective Federal Tax Rates, 1979-2005*, Congressional Budget Office, December 2007, at *http://www.cbo.gov*.

Appendix B
The Socio-Economic Dynamic:
A Conceptual View

We live in a dynamic world but our impressions of it are typically static in nature. That is, from statistics to photography, both of which are supposed to capture the way we live, we are provided, usually, with a static picture.

This paradox in our daily existence (i.e., imaging statically, but living dynamically) is paralleled by another human paradox: the way we have accumulated and organized information in order to understand ourselves and our world. We have economics, we have sociology, we have psychology, for example, in the social sciences; we have chemistry, physics, and geology in the physical sciences; and we have art, music, and literature in the domain of the arts. All of these are unique disciplines and those who practice them often take umbrage when their domains have been encroached upon. For example, economists frequently look down their noses at the sociologists if the latter attempt to become too concerned with markets, and the sociologists bristle when the economists become too engrossed in issues involving class structure. Discipline cross-over must be conducted delicately. *But*, if one asks oneself that most perplexing of all human questions, "What is life all about?" each separate and unique discipline will not take us very far.

Our knowledge of the world is, on the one hand, compartmentalized, but our lives are lived by moving (usually quickly) from one compartment to another during the course of a day or, for that matter, even an hour. After all, we go to the store, we listen to music, we spank the children, and on and on, all within short spans of time. Our lives are dynamic; only the moments within them are static. To fully understand our lives, all the disciplines must be blended together—in other words, to move from the static to the dynamic. It is *this* conceptualization that must be applied to the income distribution to fully understand it, because it is a "static" thing.

At one period in time (e.g., 1975), the income distribution looked like X and then at another period in time (e.g., 2000) it looked like Y. To understand how it changed from X to Y we have to understand the "dynamics," or the forces that produced the changes. Economics alone does not determine the shape of the income distribution at a period in time, nor is it alone responsible for its change in shape (i.e., becoming more equally distributed or less so). Any economist who is worth their salt should know this. People die, babies are born, workers go on strike, legislators increase the minimum wage, illegal immigrants cross the Rio Grande, marriages go on the rocks, and so on. There is a multiplicity of events that take place through time that exerts pressure on the income distribution and this is the socio-economic dynamic.

The discussion contained in Chapter 5 is principally concerned with how changes in the socio-economic dynamic have changed the middle class over time. But the analogy of the tectonic plates (i.e., that make up the socio-economic dynamic), cited in Chapter 4, was in the context of the overall income distribution. The social, economic, and demographic forces (some of which are identified in Chapter 5) have come together with different forces over time and have interacted with each other to different degrees.

To illustrate how the socio-economic dynamic changes over time, consider its impact on the elderly in the 1890s, 1950s, and early 2000s. One hundred or so years ago in the 1890s, someone who reached age 65 or 70 would no doubt be living with his or her children, perhaps still helping out with household chores, but dependent on the other adults of the family for his or her existence. Fifty or so years later, an elderly person more likely would be living alone (or with their spouse) and barely squeaking by on a Social Security check. In today's day and age, a senior citizen could very well be a member of an adult community, along with his or her companion, receiving Social Security, Medicare, and a private pension, and participating in the Federal government's Drug Prescription benefit program.

Clearly, the position of an elderly individual in the income distribution would have changed dramatically over 100 or so years, not only because he or she was old, but because of changes in family living arrangements, governmental programs, and improvements in medicines. More likely than not, this hypothetical elderly person would have moved considerably higher in the "static" income distribution over this period because of the different "socio-economic dynamics" (i.e., the tectonic plates) that were in operation over the last 100 years or so.

Identifying the demarcation line between the socio-economic dynamics of the 1870-1900 period and the 1900-1930 period, for example, is virtually impossible—indeed, the line is more likely to be composed of an overlapping of years. Furthermore, the specific years of the dynamics during which the major social, economic, and demographic factors were exerting their greatest influence, should only be thought of as approximations. But if anyone doubts the existence of these dynamics, all they have to do is think back across time and how life in America has changed.

Index

For Product Safety Concerns and Information please contact our EU
representative GPSR@taylorandfrancis.com Taylor & Francis Verlag GmbH,
Kaufingerstraße 24, 80331 München, Germany

Batch number: 08158437

Printed by Printforce, the Netherlands